THE UPS AND DOWNS OF
A DRIBBLY WOBBLY

THE UPS AND DOWNS OF A DRIBBLY WOBBLY

A Roller Coaster Ride Through Life With CP

Stacey Roche

With my Personal Scribbler – Fee O'Shea

First Printing: 2019
ISBN: 978-0-473-47222-1
Published by: White Rockit Books
            Tauranga – New Zealand
Cover Illustration by: CLONEMAN

White Rockit Books

For Mum and Dad.

You gave me the power, the confidence

and the strength to become who I am.

I wouldn't be the woman I am today without the two of you.

Acknowledgements

To my personal scribbler, Fee, who has guided me through the process and done an awful lot of typing.

I also want to thank LaVerne who did such a stellar job in proofing my ramblings. She definitely deserves a shout out at LaVerne Clark Editing - https://www.laverneclark.com/

Forward

Not-for-profit organisations require good people – staff, volunteers and supporters to maximize its aims and objectives. Whilst proud that the Halberg Foundation bears my name, I am mindful that many people over so many years have contributed to its growth and success.

Stacey, during her time with the Foundation was a standout, during a period of development of our services, consolidating our philosophies and defining our role in society. Personal experience in sport and life made her a strong advocate to ensure all young people have equal opportunities.

Stacey's bright and bubbly personality quickly wins friends, however this warm exterior belies a strong will to succeed whatever the challenge.

Dear friend, best wishes for your book. May it demonstrate your strengths and highlight your thoughtful effervescent disposition.

Sir Murray Halberg

Introduction

Dear Reader,

Hello. How's your day going? It's about to get a whole lot better. I thought it would be appropriate to give you a bit of a heads-up about this book.

First and foremost I want to tell you that, except for family members, all names have been changed for their own protection.

This book doesn't conform to the norm, just like I don't. What I mean by this is that it's about my life but not necessarily laid out in sequential order. It's a selection of notable events that have occurred which has shaped my attitude, my drive and both my light and dark humour.

So, Reader, jump around this book and enjoy.

Stacey.
The original Dribbly Wobbly.

1.

IN THE BEGINNING

The Start

I guess we'll start at the beginning simply because it's a good place to start.

I was born in New Zealand and the doctors weren't really sure about my prognosis so gave Mum and Dad three options of what may happen:

1. I might not live.

2. I may have a disability.

3. I may be perfectly okay

Once they knew that I had a significant impairment, they suggested I would be better off in an institution. Their logic being that Mum and Dad could get on with their lives without the burden of taking care of a child with a real significant impairment.

Mum and Dad told the Doctors that their baby girl was perfect in their eyes. They would certainly do all that they could to give her a good life with the love and security every child deserves. Thank goodness they did because who knows what my life would be like now. Probably rocking in a corner somewhere in an institution.

I was extremely fortunate to get the right, defiant parents whose example of giving the figurative finger to the doctors that day set me on my path doing likewise to people who hinder my progress.

I'm the youngest of three. My brother and sister are four years older and they are twins. Mum and Dad planned me as they just wanted to have a nice, easy, single child after a pretty full-on time of it with the twins, whom they'd had when they were still very young.

BOOM – then I happened … kinda messed that idea up!!!

At five months the diagnosis came through that I had Cerebral Palsy, or CP as it's known in the cool circles, or Dribbly Wobbly in the really cool circles. In 1978 there was not a lot of information given to families, so it was a real case of figuring it out as you went along.

For those of you who aren't familiar with cerebral palsy, I'll paint you a wee picture. There was a long-held view that CP was caused by lack of oxygen during the birthing process, however, that belief has since been debunked and the thinking nowadays is that CP happens actually in utero at any given time. CP is a very unique impairment and presents itself in different ways for each person. For me, however, the true impact wasn't known until I wasn't achieving the milestones associated with infancy such as sitting, crawling and talking.

Once I got out of the infant stage, my inquisitive nature made me figure out a way of getting from A to B. I developed strategies to allow me to achieve my goals on my own terms. This happened to start with 'knee walking' which I soon became very adept at. However, it wasn't so great for the knees.

Mum and Dad very quickly became great problem solvers with all the issues that came with me. They invested in kneepads, which made my life so much more comfortable, and as a bonus, my speed increased. You see, even from a small age my need for speed was evident.

The next great piece of equipment I got was a giant pushchair. Imagine, Reader, one of those old-fashioned, canvas slung easy fold type of toddler pushchair but just double in size. I thought I was the Queen of the Castle! This cool blue and white striped pushchair gave all of us much more freedom when we went out and about.

Off to Primary School

Getting into primary school proved to be the start of many battles that my family and I had to wage in order to overcome prejudice, ignorance and downright fear of a Dribbly Wobbly. Mum and Dad obviously wanted me to go to the country primary school in the little town where we lived because my siblings went there.

The principal at the time flat out refused to take the 'crippled' child because that wasn't where 'crippled' children went ... they went on a bus to the city to go to a 'special' school.

For Mum and Dad, this was non-negotiable. So, they lobbied intensively and finally when resorting to the threat of legal action, the principle relented. So, when I turned five, I rocked up to the school in my giant, blue and white striped pushchair and it was a fait accompli.

Soon after I started the principal who had told me I wasn't welcome 'retired' ... and our second battle was won.

When I got to school I was either having to be pushed, or with my kneepads on, knee-walk around. However, it wasn't long before I realised that to keep up with my mates I needed to get up off my backside. That need for speed kicked in again.

Up till then, I hadn't really given any thought to walking; I didn't need to, so therefore, it wasn't a priority. But at school, I could see my friends having so much more fun on their feet than I did on my knees and that was the motivation I needed to get me up.

Walking wasn't the only skill I needed to keep up with my friends. I had arrived at school with very limited language but soon realised that communicating my thoughts and needs were hugely beneficial.

The ability to speak is one of the fundamental skills you need to make friends, to be able to learn at school and just to be able to tell the teacher the basics like, "Please, Miss, can I go to the toilet?"

The use of language defines intelligence and how you use that language indicates your level. I think I learnt quite early on that it was a vital component of my arsenal to ensure that people knew I was a damn sight brighter than I appeared to be.

The gap between my peers and me was quite minimal in the early years, so it was easy to make friends because I could keep up. However, this all changed later on.

A couple of years into school I got my second assisted device. This was an awkward walker with only two wheels at the front and a push and drag technique was required. Because it was such a terrible design, the wheels at the front would always dig into the uneven surfaces outside making the walker stop suddenly and propelling me over the top and face planting me onto the asphalt.

I soon realised that it was holding me back.
What did I do? Well, I just picked it up and carried it because it was faster!

I better point out now that I come from a very sporty family. My dad was an elite athlete in his chosen sport of Olympic style wrestling. So naturally, I was strongly encouraged to do everything and anything I could in sport.

Going to a mainstream school made it more challenging to compete with my non-disabled peers. This more often than not resulted in me finishing last at everything. However, because I saw myself as equal to my peers, I always held myself to their standard, which enabled me to constantly strive for success. I am 100 percent certain that attending a mainstream school and having non happy-clappy parents is what has given me my core values.

The 'coming last' really didn't affect me so much in the early days because it was more about having fun, but later on my desire to win kicked in.

The Great Race

I have never forgotten an awesome teacher I had at primary school that I think changed my attitude to sport. He got the balance between competitiveness and fun just right for me, which had never been done before.

The best example of this was the cross-country event. He designed and constructed a mirror image course specifically for me. He figured out from my ability that the length of my course needed to be a certain distance so I would finish around about the middle of the pack.

The cross-country day came. All the parents rocked on up to see their darlings compete including my parents. I distinctly remember the starting gun going off because it gave me such a massively huge fright that I fell over.

I quickly got myself up and started to run the race. I could see my peers jumping over the stiles and going through the paddocks. My course was flat but just as challenging.

Halfway through I looked around and figured that if I pulled my finger out I could actually be up in the top group. Man, I felt good. I saw my parents in the crowd and their cheers spurred me on. I was invincible and nothing was in my way. I was not disabled now. I was Stacey the runner, not Stacey the Dribbly Wobbly.

The end of my course merged into the main course. This had been the teacher's number one priority and he'd been adamant that I would finish the race with everyone else.

As I rounded the last corner I could see the finish line and the tape was still intact, which meant I was in the lead. I quickly looked around and saw some of my class gaining on me.

'Don't fall over, don't fall over' was running through my head 'I've got this, I can do it'.

Just as I reached the tape I did the Hollywood dive and propelled myself across the line, breaking the tape, and coming in as the winner. Never in my wildest dreams did I ever think I would run and win a cross-country with my non-disabled peers.

Best sporting achievement ever … up to that date!

Some of the parents were not happy with the result because they thought I had been given too much of an advantage. However, all of my peers were thrilled that I'd won because they had been there right from the beginning, seen my progress and the remarkable change in my ability.

That experience really shaped the way I valued myself and how my peers valued me. And I think, looking back, that was the beginning of my sporting career. I then started to believe I could succeed.

Saying that – I still finished last in pretty much everything in secondary school, but my dad was adamant that I was to do everything alongside my peers, so I did. It was hard at the time, but it gave me the desire to succeed that I have to this day.

The Wizard of Oz Play

I was eleven and our primary school was putting on a huge production of the Wizard of Oz. Everyone in my class and the class below had the opportunity to have a part in this production.

When I got to pick my role, I'm sure the teachers had a sharp intake of breath when I said I wanted to be a ballerina.

I got my wish and ballerina it was.

Rehearsals started and it soon became apparent that they would need to modify my part in the choreography as I kept falling over and disrupting the other dancers.

The idea was that the dancers were the tornado and were running in a rhythmic circle ... except me. So after it became obvious that I couldn't exactly run gracefully in the circle, the dance teacher put me into the middle of the tornado where I would beautifully pirouette like a true ballerina. The middle of a tornado is called the 'Eye of the Storm' how appropriate!

After a term of rehearsals, we were ready and the two nights the show was going to be on were completely sold out.
Mum and Dad decided to come on closing night as they figured I would have it perfect by then.
Opening night went like a charm. I had my beautiful pink ballerina costume of leotard and tutu on, the first and only time I've ever worn a tutu. Make-up and hair were perfect. I felt like such a star.
The pirouetting went like clockwork and I was incredibly proud to be a real ballerina. What a great show.

Set the scene: Closing night. Raining. Super excited to be performing in front of my family.

Mum and Dad dropped me off near the hall and went off to park the car. Now I was quite independently walking at that time, so because it was raining and I was excited, I made the decision to run (my way) into the hall so I wouldn't get too wet.

Bad decision! As the floor at the beginning of the hall was wet, you guessed it, I slipped and fell … SMACK! A dramatic face plant onto the foyer floor.

The teachers rushed to my aid and helped me up. I was sore and it was discovered later that I was concussed, but I was adamant that I was going to perform.

They put my costume on and tried to cover the lump on my head with make-up. This was going to happen! I couldn't let my mum and dad down.
I was put into a quiet room as the music was hurting my head (that should have been a clue), then it was my turn to tread the boards and be a star. The teachers came and helped me to the back of the stage ready to go on.

Suddenly and violently I vomited, like projectile. It went everywhere and the poor ballerinas had to tippy-toe around the mess I'd created.

Ten seconds later my intro music started. My heart broke as I had done all this work to show my parents how perfect I was and the moment was snatched from me. I saw my career as a ballet dancer getting mopped away with the vomit. What a train wreck!

My parents were pulled out of the audience and I was bundled into the car and taken home.

That night Mum was tucking me in and I asked her, "Am I ever going to be better?"
I can't remember what she said, however, she has since told me that that was one of the most difficult moments she had as a mother.

This is one of many, many stories of me being concussed. I'm actually surprised that I'm not more damaged than I am because of the number of head blows I've had in my life and continue to have. Why, I fell just the other day, Reader, and whacked my head which resulted in seven stitches and concussion.

Mum and I were having a heart to heart conversation recently and she told me that she was certain each time I fell it was going to be the one that killed me. Learning this did make me feel awful that I have, and continue to, put my parents through such traumatic experiences. I could never imagine always having that hanging over my child.
Having said that, they never let their fear colour my experiences and I was always encouraged to play hard and fast, just the way I liked it and still do.

God Will Heal You.

Seven-year-olds are very impressionable and this became apparent when I went to stay with a school friend and her family.

This friend of mine had recently moved away from our town, therefore we were really missing each other. Our mothers organised for me to go and stay with her and her family for a whole week. It was exciting, and I looked forward to seeing my friend again and spending time with her.
We knew that the family was religious and that I would be expected to attend their church. And, although my family were not church-going people, Mum and Dad always encouraged us to experience new things so we could make up our own mind on how we viewed the world. This was just another opportunity.

Towards the end of the holiday, my friend's parents started talking to me about the 'wonder of God' and if I was a true believer, I would be able to speak in tongues of which I never understood nor mastered. Looking back, this was ironic considering my speech was already weird and I wouldn't have thought it was too far off their idea of tongues.

According to these two fundamental psychopaths, the purpose of speaking in tongues and having complete faith was that God would heal me!!! So what I must do is,
"Pray to the Lord every night and he will heal you."

As a seven-year-old, I completely believed them and went about 'religiously' praying to this great God to heal me. I had taken the whole thing literally and was excited about getting rid of my CP and being a normal little girl. Each night in bed I prayed … hard! And continued this when I returned home.

One night, Mum came in to find me engrossed in my praying and she asked me what I was doing. I explained to her that God would heal me if I prayed hard enough.

She never showed anger and was so gentle in telling me that, "This praying gig won't take it away. Your CP is here to stay, it's what makes you perfect in my eyes so you don't need to wish it gone".
My mum had such a beautiful way of explaining stuff like this to me.

I stopped the praying.
The 'religious' experience I had back then has coloured the way I view religion even to this day. I'm very sceptical and suspicious when people approach me to talk about the good Lord. In fact, even just the mention of the word 'God' I want to run a mile, which is very hard to do when you're in my shoes … my shoes are definitely not running shoes!

A few friendships have ended because of their need to convert me and my absolute resistance and horror at being converted.

I'm not an atheist, far from it. I'm spiritual and believe in a higher power.

Support Apparatus

As I have wandered through life, I've had different pieces of equipment to help me independently get about. The giant pushchair, already mentioned, came first. Then, when I started walking, callipers were introduced to give me more stability. All I can remember about the callipers was that they were freakin' hot and heavy, and I had to wear boots with them ... think Forest Gump ... that was me. However, they did the job and soon I didn't require them any more.

Next came the push/drag walker, soon followed by a bike with training wheels then a massive three-wheeler that kept on tipping over because I'd go round the corners too fast. (Had a few injuries on that puppy). At last came my fantastic, recumbent, three-wheeler, Roche the Rebel, which followed me from school to university.

I was actually able to walk independently of these devices; they were just there to get me around faster.

So this was how my life began, some experiences good and some bad. However, it did set me up with a fundamental self-belief that held me in good stead as I continued the roller-coaster ride of my life.

2.

FAMILY LIFE

We were (and still are), an active family. Just because you've got a Dribbly Wobbly in the mix doesn't stop you from doing anything. That was my mum and dad's wonderful philosophy.

How A CP Hikes

Dad had bought a baby backpack so I could go on hikes with my family. As I got older and struggled to fit, my dad pulled it apart and welded it back together fashioning it into more of a seat. Of course, there was ongoing panel beating done as I grew but finally we had to say goodbye to that mode of transport and I ended up riding on my dad's shoulders.

Now, this wasn't as easy as it seems. Having no balance and no seat belt makes for a scary ride and there were times when I would rock backwards making my dad nearly lose his balance. As a wrestler, he was very agile and strong, but my unsolicited movements would make this a real challenge for him.

Sitting still for a Dribbly Wobbly is really hard but sitting still on a five foot eight inch (1.77 metre) man who was bounding up mountains and over valleys was nigh on impossible. It took all my concentration and energy to do so.

One particular hike was up a fairly tough hill. We got to the top and as I got down from Dad's shoulders I said, "Whew, that was hard work."

Mum and Dad looked at each other in utter bemusement as they were both sweating profusely.

"Hard?" Mum exclaimed "You've been sitting the whole way Dad's the one who's done the hard work."

Let me point out here that my parents were young and information about cerebral palsy was not readily accessed. So little did they know that I had been fighting the whole way against gravity and my spazziness just to keep still.

Grandparents.

I was so blessed to have my paternal grandmother until I was twenty two years old, and my maternal grandparents until I was thirty eight years old. I was extremely close to all three of these people and in one way or another they influenced my life and gave me so much with their wisdom and their love.

Rani and Poppa, My Maternal Grandparents.

In my early years, Rani and Poppa lived in Raglan, a small seaside town on the west coast of the North Island, famous for its black sand and great surf. But for me, it is synonymous with 'Raglan trees' and 'Raglan birds'. Okay so they're only the classic tall palm trees and seagulls, but Rani and Poppa made them so much more than what they really are. This is the magic of grandparents.

As a kid when we drove through and got to the 'Raglan trees', we knew the journey was just about over. It was a long and winding trip from one side of the coast to the other but the reward was worth it to get to see Rani and Poppa.

They lived in a cool brick home with a huge backyard. Inside was warm and comfy, and I loved the bright red wall in the lounge. This epitomised them, as they were really vibrant, loving and fun to be with.

We would walk from their place down to the neighbours, who had a candyfloss machine. If I walked the whole way, which was a real challenge for me, the candyfloss was my reward. Bribery and corruption were paramount and worked every time. (I loved that candyfloss.)

Just like the 'Raglan' birds and trees, my names for stuff were not the most original. Another example was the famous Whale Bay known for its great swells creating phenomenal surf that riders from all around the world come to. Well, I called that 'Rocky Beach' … hey, it had lots of rocks, and I never saw a whale there.

As a family, we'd go to Rocky Beach and over many rocks we went with me being totally oblivious to the hard work this entailed just getting me there. But they never let on and it was such a magical experience for me.

I remember climbing over the big boulders and then paddling in the rock pools, finding crabs, starfish, and shrimps and making jewellery with Neptune's Necklace. How lucky was I not to have to think about the logistics, but merely just enjoy the rewards.

Rani and Poppa left Raglan and went to manage a kiwifruit orchard in the Bay of Plenty, which provided new experiences, fun exploring, and playing under the many pergolas and vines.

One particular activity that both my brother and I loved was 'dragging'.

Let me explain 'dragging'. Poppa had a tractor and to start with he tied a rope to the back and attached a sack, which my brother and I used to sit on. Hanging on tight, Poppa would then proceed to drive the tractor round in one big paddock with the intention of trying to get us to fall off.
It soon became apparent, as the injuries increased, that a change in design was needed.

Mark II saw a bigger rubber mat with a raised wooden front for bracing our feet on and a good rope handle. But, not only was the equipment upgraded, so too was what we wore. Now it was serious. Dressed head-to-toe in protective clothing, we were ready for battle. One particular corner was so intense that we nicknamed it the 'Corner of Death' and I'd scream to my brother, "Oh no!!! Here comes the corner of death!"

It got us every time.

Rani and Poppa remained on that orchard until they retired and shifted to Katikati where they built a home on Mum and Dad's property. It was wonderful to have them so close.

Nanny, My Paternal Grandmother.

When I was little Nanny lived in Hamilton, some distance away, but still close enough to visit. Nanny had something like twenty grandchildren when I was a child and even more when I got older, but she always made me feel like I was her favourite when I was in her presence. I've spoken to many of my cousins about this and they have said exactly the same thing they thought they were her favourite. What a beautiful trait to have to be able to show each one of us such individual precious attention. I suppose she was used to this having nine children of her own.

Nanny moved to Picton, the top of the South Island, which meant that spending time with her was very precious.

My brother and I flew down by ourselves for a visit when I was around ten years old. My first plane ride, so exciting, and naturally I had to visit the toilet to steal all the soaps and stuff. Unfortunately, I locked myself in, and my brother had to come to my rescue. Needless to say, I was too embarrassed to walk out with stolen soap.

We arrived in one piece and the holiday started. My cousin had joined us, and on one particular day, Nanny took us off for a day trip to the snow. This was my first encounter with snow. Snow and I didn't really work that well together as it was absolutely freezing plus I couldn't walk that well in it, so Nanny and I spent the day in the car with the heater on full blast. I reckon I got the better deal because not only was I warm but I had precious one-on-one time with Nanny.

Although I didn't see as much of Nanny as I would have liked to, I know I was her favourite, and I don't care what the rest of the family say!

What Do Neil Diamond, Corduroy Pants and Horses Have in Common?

The answer? ... I dislike them all immensely!

With the best intentions, Mum and Dad discovered and enrolled me in riding school for disabled people. This was intended to be my Saturday morning sport just like my siblings had theirs.
As this school was about an hour's drive away, my parents teamed up with another family of a child who had an intellectual impairment so that the parents could take turns in driving us to the 'sport'.

A pair of corduroy trousers was my mum's choice of dress code for me. I don't know quite what it was about them, but my dislike for them has developed so much over time that now I can't even bear to touch the fabric.

On the days that the boy's mother took us, I became quite carsick. I was always put in the back seat as the boy was in the front with his mum. As a result, this made the carsickness worse and I came to really dread these trips.

But that wasn't as bad as when his Mum would play Neil Diamond non-stop an hour each way with the volume turned up. So, in my corduroys and listening to Neil Diamond I would hang my head out the window wishing that I was anywhere but there.

I would get my revenge on the alternative weeks when Mum drove as it was then me in the front, no Neil Diamond, didn't feel sick BUT still had to wear the corduroy pants, and still had to tolerate the dosey horses that were at the school.

The actual 'sport' of this type of horse riding was designed to cater to people with significantly more physical and intellectual impairments than I had which explained the dosey horses.

Most of the children didn't even get on a horse but spent the two hours just patting them. I did ride the horses but I wanted to trot or gallop and do cool stuff like the real equestrians I had seen on TV. However, as the horses we rode were one trot away from the dog food processing plant it meant the whole thing was slow, tedious, and incredibly boring.

The intensity of these three things … the horse, Neil Diamond and corduroys, has haunted me throughout my life. To the point that my work colleagues designed a birthday card one year for me. It was spectacular in its design and message. There was Neil Diamond's head on a body with a corduroy jacket riding a ginormous horse. I had to hand it to them; they knew me so well!

Mum and Dad's intention was always to give me all the opportunities that they could and horse riding sounded like another great one. How wrong they were.

To this day:

I don't like the feel of corduroy.

I can't stand listening to Neil Diamond,

and

I loathe horses!

Abandonment Issues.

When I was ten years old I was referred to a residential facility to be assessed in terms of equipment and anything else that might help me in school. This residential school is for children with physical and intellectual impairments. It's in Auckland, the largest New Zealand city about a three-hour drive from where we lived.

Because it was an intensive assessment, Mum and I were required to stay there for a week. When we arrived, we settled into a unit which was part of the complex. Each day, I would go to the school either to go to classes or have numerous assessments from the many professionals who were there.

Every lunchtime I would head back to the unit where Mum and I would have lunch together, and I would tell her about my morning.

One day, I arrived at our unit to find that Mum wasn't there.

My immediate reaction was that she had gone, gone forever and that I would never see her or my family ever again.

Talk about being melodramatic but this was a suspicion of mine from early days, that Mum and Dad would get rid of me because I was too much hard work.

I had been keeping pretty much to myself up till then so there was only one thing to do.

I headed back and started making friends with some of the residents of the school. I knew who the 'top dogs' were so I knew who I had to buddy up with in order to be looked after as this was going to be my future. (Great learning if ever I was to find myself in prison!)

Later in the day, the teacher took me back to the unit. Imagine my surprise when I saw Mum there. I hugged her the tightest I'd ever done and then said, "Why are you here?"

She was quite surprised and taken aback by my reaction. She didn't realise the ripple effect of just being late home from shopping would have on the mind of a little ten-year-old who was already suspicious about being at this facility. What was a minor thing in her world was a catastrophic event in mine. The end of my family as I knew it or so I had thought.

I really was quite surprised that Mum and Dad wanted to keep me, as in my mind, this was a prime opportunity to relieve themselves of this burden they had to endure.

I don't think I really articulated to my mum how it had impacted on me until many years later when I recalled the experience. She was absolutely heartbroken that I had even considered my family would ever walk away from me because that was the furthermost thing from my mum and dad's thoughts.

From that moment on I knew I was an integral part of a powerfully loving family that would always be forever connected.

The Rose Incident

Mum and Dad went away for a night and left me in the capable care of my sister and brother. Now, what do you think a couple of young teenagers do? Have a party, of course.

Everyone rocked up and the party started. How buzzy was it for me because my siblings were sooooooo cool and so were their friends. My ego was definitely high as everyone took an interest in me, perhaps too much so.

It wasn't long before I was under the table and the teenagers were topping up my sipper bottle with homebrew.

Being part of this party was my reward for keeping quiet. However, they got busted anyway, but not by anything I said.

It turned out that someone at the party stole some roses from a neighbour's garden. So when Mum and Dad got home the neighbour arrived and said that they didn't mind us having a party, but were very upset that one of the guests had raided their rose garden.

We pointed the finger at one of my sister's girlfriends (blonde and future head girl at the high school). Of course, she swore black and blue that she didn't do it. But to this day, we harken back to the 'rose incident' telling people to hide all the flora whenever she is around.

The Rock is Going to Fall on Us

This is a story about a song and singing and family times and love.

It starts when I was young, seven, I think. Dad bought a cassette tape (yes, that's how old I am), of Harry Chapin … don't worry, if you haven't heard of him, nobody has apart from the Roches.

Whenever we went on a road trip, which was quite often, Dad would put the tape in, and I'd listen intently to one particular song that scared and fascinated me at the same time, 'The Rock'. (Google the lyrics sometime, Reader, it's quite a tale).

So whenever we drove through gorges, of which there are quite a few here in New Zealand, we would ask Dad if there were any rocks that were going to fall on us.

The song had made its impact.

Even to this day, that song is still in the Roche family.

So in 2000, my dad's beautiful mother passed away, and at her funeral the family decided that we didn't want to see each other only on sad occasions. That's when 'Whanau Idol' was born. (Whanau is Maori for family). Now, Dad is one of nine children, six are girls and all have beautiful voices, so naturally, singing is an integral part of the family.

All the Roches meet every two years. What a party, the highlight being the Karaoke on the Saturday night. It has got so competitive that we actually bring in neutral judges with no family affiliations.

The prize is hugely sought after. Polished paua shells are awarded to the best in different categories ... yes, there are categories ... this is serious!

Now strategy is also employed in this competition especially when you have no singing talent like myself. However, one year I asked four of the cousins and aunties to join me. Unbeknown to them, I had selected them because they had the best voices. I made sure that I stayed out of range of the microphone. My performance as a lip-syncing singer rivalled that of Milli Vanilli (I was heartbroken when I discovered they were phonies). The other key strategy that I employed was selecting the amazing 'Hallelujah' song ... how can you not love that?

Sure enough, victory was ours and I came home with my polished paua - a cherished prize that sits on my bench to this day.

Back to the rock song. On one of these weekends I discovered that it was not only my family but indeed, it was the entire Roche clan that knew and loved the 'The Rock'. Over the years it has become a bit of an anthem. We all sing it with gusto and now we've also brought in hand and arm choreography to tell the story more effectively.

3.

IS IT GUNNA HURT?

Hospitals I Have Known

As a child I had many, many hospital visits where they would X-ray me, look at the way I walked and my physical abilities.

I didn't really mind these visits, as there wasn't anything medically invasive about them and I could have a day off school.

However.

I was at that young age where I'd become aware of my body like many little girls do. So to have to remove my clothes and walk around with just my knickers and underwear top on was embarrassing.

This was heightened when more doctors, mainly males, came in to watch and I got the sense that I was just an interesting case study, especially when a doctor would call out to a colleague,
"(*insert name here*), come in and look at this one."

There was never anything dodgy that happened and my mum was always with me the whole time, but it was just a feeling of vulnerability and that my body was there for their education and I wasn't a real person.

That was one type of hospital visit. The other type was the numerous admissions for concussion, which I have already alluded to.

Actually being admitted wasn't the problem; it was during the night that really sucked. The nurses would come in to take my vitals and because I was concussed, they would wake me up to make sure I was alive and coherent.

Have you ever had your eyelid pulled up and a torchlight shone into your eye when you were sound asleep? Well, that's what they did. But wait, not just once, every couple of hours throughout the night. And they would ask me inane questions to go with it and would wonder why I was slow to answer at three o'clock in the morning.

"Where are you?" "What day is it?" "What's your name?"

Honestly, I just wanted to tell them to go away and let me sleep.

It is interesting to note that I have recently experienced concussion and so prepared myself for these nightly intrusions when I was admitted. I was pleasantly surprised when the nurse put a clip on my finger, to record my vitals. No stupid questions were asked and no beam of light from torches on the eyeballs.

Science has come a long way since I was a kid. Apparently, the old way of doing things was never satisfactory and the results were usually compromised as they figured that a person, in the middle of the night, might not be totally compos mentis with or without a concussion.

One hospital visit actually was a lifesaver. Not literally but figuratively as if it hadn't occurred, I would have died a social death.

When I was sixteen, I had a shoulder injury that wasn't going away. The last resort was to operate and the operation was scheduled at the same time as my first ever school ball.
This so worked in my favour as I had no friends and definitely no date and I was not looking forward to this ball at all. The only time I was grateful for a hospital visit.

Not only did I go to hospital in New Zealand. Oh no, I am a hospital globetrotter.
Strap yourself in, Reader, this is a doozie.

Bali Belly

Ringo, my partner at the time, and I were living together in Auckland during the Rugby World Cup that was held in New Zealand. We decided to take the opportunity of renting out my home as it was within walking distance to one of the main rugby grounds.

We then took off on a month-long holiday to Bali. Why Bali? Why not?

The first three weeks were wonderful, filled with cocktails, cheap massages and lots of adventures. The last week, however, was the week from hell.

It started out with just a rotten headache. We'd organised a tour guide to take us around the Island and to go snorkelling. He arrived to pick us up, and after downing some headache tablets, I thought I'd be fine.

By the time we got to the beach to go snorkelling my headache was still there and had actually gotten worse. I decided to stay in the car and have a sleep and let Ringo have the adventure without me.

On the way back, the driver said he knew where we could go to 'fix' this. He stopped at a pharmacy type shop and on telling the 'pharmacist' my symptoms, we left with a bottle of pills. I later discovered they were very powerful antibiotics that should never have been dished out to me. Dodgy eh?

The next day the headache was still there, but the symptoms had progressed to include a case of mild diarrhoea about ten minutes after eating anything.

I toughed it out for two days. I was on holiday, for heaven's sake I didn't want to be sick. I was in paradise and I needed to make the most of it! However, it was not to be.

By day three the action had really heated up and had evolved into a gastro emergency with me vomiting and having full-on diarrhoea. It was decided that I should go to the hospital.

I went to the BMIC hospital, which had been built by the Australians after the horrendous Bali Bombing. It is state of the art and is still run by Australian medical professionals. I was quickly seen by a doctor who then proceeded to order an urgent ultrasound. The results came back showing an intestinal parasite … ewww YUK where had that come from??
I was then admitted to a ward, where I grossed out the other patients with bouts of violent and noisy vomiting.
After a couple of days it started to come right so I was discharged and we went back to the hotel.

However, it was not over.

The very next day I was worse than ever, doubled over in pain, crazy headache and vomiting everything. What went down, came right back up again, even water. So it was back to the hospital.

Another ultrasound discovered that the parasite had gone but before it had left it had damaged my pancreas that resulted in pancreatitis. Damn, this was getting serious.

I was in there for a further five days, and this time, I had my own room. I slept most of it. We had medical insurance, thank goodness (all up it cost about $35k). I was released on the Saturday morning, which as it turned out, was forty-eight hours before I could have been medivaced home. (Keep this in mind, Reader, as you continue on).

I was still not feeling the best when I was discharged, but we were to fly home the next day, and all I wanted to do was get home and see Mum and Dad. They had actually offered to fly out earlier that week but I told them not to come as I knew it would have been crazy expensive even though I really wished they would.

We arrived at the airport and I was under instructions from the hospital to take a cocktail of drugs just before my flight, which I dutifully did.

As we got to the departure lounge, I started to feel sick. Oh, no … here it comes again! Clutching a sick bag, I started vomiting just as the pilot and cabin crew walked past. I heard the pilot say to the ground crew, "She's not getting on my flight."

I stopped vomiting, but the damage had already been done and no amount of pleading or showing medical documents would get me on this flight. You see, I also had track marks and plasters on my arms from the drips I'd had and these made it look like I was a right druggy.

I will never forget the room full of people with their boarding passes ready as I was wheeled through the middle of them all. Glaring passengers. You couldn't really blame them, I was going to be holding up their flight as our luggage had to be off-loaded.

Oh, where was the medivac!

We got back to the hotel, and the staff there couldn't have been sweeter. I must add here that they had sent me flowers when I was in hospital. They were mortified that I had got so sick while being a guest with them.

That reminds me, the nurses in the hospital were the most amazing and loveliest people in the world and I remain Facebook friends with a lot of them to this day.

Back to the drama.

I was determined to get home. The next day I made sure I didn't have the particular cocktail of drugs and I wore a long-sleeve top to cover the evidence. As we got to the airport Ringo kept hissing at me things like:

"Keep it together."

"Don't show them that you're sick."

"We've got to get on the plane."

"Once we're in the air, you can vomit your heart out!"

So, keep it together I did, and as soon as we took off, out came the bag, and I allowed myself to vomit violently. But, not to be outdone, the lady sitting next to me also decided to vomit, and we took turns all the way to Melbourne. Unfortunately, we were delayed in Melbourne for seven hours, which resulted in me lying on the floor interwoven with rushing to the toilet every so often.

Finally, we got home and the "Kia Ora, welcome to New Zealand" voice rang out as we came into the Auckland International Airport. That was enough to get me to burst into tears, and they continued until I was in my mum's arms.

Nothing quite beats your Mum.

It did take me about six months to get over this. In fact, I had to take quite a lot of time off work and then only part-time until I recovered my strength. The fatigue was the worst part of the aftermath of this debilitating Bali adventure.

I'm Falling . . .

One of the things in my life that drives me nuts is the fact that I spontaneously FALL.

Absolutely no reason ... no warning ... I just FALL.

Anyone who knows me knows that I'm a person who loves to be in control. I pride myself on my organisational skills, which has led to a very enjoyable life. I like to be in a routine and know what's around the corner.

And I definitely don't bring a FALL into any equation!!!!!

Spontaneously falling is detrimental to my health.

I just need to trip and the result = hospital.

Especially as I get older I'm noticing that I don't bounce as much as I used to. What I mean is that I used to fall, get up, brush myself off, and carry on. Now when I fall there are consequences.

The last thought that goes through my head when I am falling is 'this is going to hurt' and most often … it does!!!

But now that I'm a grown-up, it's frowned upon to wail and hysterically scream for my mum even though that's all I want to do.

Aside from the fact that I can sustain some pretty nasty injuries, it really riles me because it upsets my whole routine and I have to reschedule my calendar and get the bloodstains out of the carpet.

Call in forensics, a massacre just happened.

Let's get one thing straight, CP is not degenerative. However, as I get older, I have noticed that things are getting increasingly harder, and when I do fall, it's a bit more dramatic.

In these falls I have hit:

Front of the head – side of the head – back of the head and just about every other part of the body. I'm amazed I'm still alive.

The other day I was watching a TV programme and this dude was running, tripped, and hit his head on the corner of the coffee table, and died ... like, dead ... straight away!
My brain went into overload and I was on the phone to Mum immediately saying, "I could die!!!!" Her response was, "It's TV luv, and anyway, you've got the toughest head I know." Thanks, Mum, you can still make it all better.

4.

FRIENDS

In the early days, friends were easy to make because I was a cute little blondie who just wanted to have fun. However, as I got older, the gap became wider in physical ability, and making friends was a lot harder to achieve simply because I couldn't keep up with them.

I did all I could to be part of the crowd, even to the extent that when I was about ten years old, I joined in with the cool girls who were smoking cigars in the school toilets. I was so stoked to be included but only managed a couple of puffs before we were busted and sent to the principal's office. This was the first and only time I was sent there and it made me feel very guilty and ashamed. You see, try as I might to fit into the 'cool' crowd, I really was a good girl at heart.

The punishment was to write an apology letter and get our parents to sign it. This was one of the hardest conversations I had with my mum, and I begged and begged her not to tell my dad, cause I was sure he would have ripped my head off!!!

I remember my sixth form year (seventeen years old), was particularly tough. I didn't fit into any of the groups at school. I was left behind in sport, and my academic prowess was limited to having a person help me take notes, which was another barrier to overcome.

I became quite clever and adept at hiding my loneliness and my friendlessness. I would eat my lunch in the toilets so no one would see me eating alone. I knew this wasn't right but it was the only way I could, I thought, maintain my credibility because if no one saw me by myself, no one would know I was by myself.

I then progressed my invisibility by going to my grandparents for lunches as they lived right on the edge of the college. And this is where I spent most of my sixth form year and the beginning of my seventh form. However, Dad busted me one day and told me that this wasn't the way to spend adolescence. He acknowledged that it would be hard, but in the long run, having friends my own age would be best.

Unbeknown to me, he also got the principal involved, and the principal held a special assembly with all the seventh formers (without me) and told them that they needed to pick up their game and include me. I only found this out many years later in a pub, with a few drinks under my belt, catching up with some schoolmates.

So, I was then forced to sit in the common room at interval and lunchtime and try and look cool. I did this by buying a Cleo magazine and sitting on a table ... sorry, *tangata o te whenua*.

Now, let me draw you a picture. In my last year at college (seventh form), there was a natural divide between two groups; the cool kids and the nerdy kids.

The nerdy kids listened to the principal a lot more, and slowly but surely, I was adopted into their group, which was ironic considering the fact that I was a bit of a dummy, or that's how I thought of myself.

I have wonderful memories of my seventh form year and am so grateful for the meddling that both my dad and the principal did on my behalf.
I hosted the pre-ball party at my place and even had a date for the ball. This was a tenuous title as we had the obligatory photo at the start and I never saw him again ... like ... ever!!!

Roche the Rebel

'Roche the Rebel' was born in secondary school thanks to a contact of my dad who hooked me up with a pretty sweet recumbent trike. Thanks also need to go to the local Lions Club and Halberg Trust for sponsoring the purchase of this trike.
Before Roche the Rebel, I was riding a giant trike that I kept tipping over, and as there were no helmets in those days, kept sending me to hospital with head injuries.
The Rebel (the brand name of the trike) transformed the way I got around, and speed was definitely my power. 'Roche the Rebel' was the name people called my beast machine and me.

One day, the name appeared on the back of the trike, thanks to our awesome art teacher, and from that day on, it was painted into my history.

What I lacked on foot I made up for tenfold on that Rebel. Oh, how I loved it. It opened up such freedom and many opportunities. It also meant I could finally keep up with my peers and even beat them.

I have been told that I was regarded as a danger by the younger kids because I would set my sights on getting from A to B, and if someone was in my way … tough, I'd just plough right on through!

The last day of school in seventh form is such a big deal, and there's always a champagne breakfast held somewhere. In my year, it was held at one of the 'cool' kid's houses, and us 'nerds' (or as I like to say "the intelligent ones plus me"), were actually invited for the first time during that entire year.
Unbeknown to me, the cool kids dared each other to try and get me as drunk as they could. And, because I wasn't used to being courted by all the cool kids, I happily obliged and became a paralytic drunk by the time the school bell went.

As we drove into the school gates, the principal stormed out of the office and said very loudly, "If any of you are drunk, you will be expelled and your Bursary mark will be null and void."

I was so inebriated that I did not heed this warning but my mates (the true ones), carried me into the common room where I rolled up in a ball in the corner and promptly went to sleep.

They knew that they had to get me out of the school before the principal found me so they smuggled me out and delivered me to my mother who put me to bed.

When the principal called out my name at the final assembly to a few giggles, he figured out what had happened but didn't pursue it.

I never really appreciated this principal and all he did for me until later when I invited him to my university graduation, and I then understood what a true, kind man he really is.

Look, No Hands . . . Showing Off

My ankle was playing up quite a bit so it was decided that I should have it put into a cast for about eight weeks ... yes, eight very long weeks!

I had to give up Roche the Rebel and 'trade it in' for a dingy, ugly fat wheelchair given to me by the hospital. Now, this was the first time I had been in a wheelchair full-time, and to say I didn't like it is a huge understatement.

It was the first time (sad to say of many), that I had my independence taken away, and I had to rely completely on other people to get me where I wanted to go.

My brother and sister were tasked with pushing me to school each morning, and my parents had organised for me to have a volunteer from my last class each day to leave early in order to push me home and then get back to school in time for the final bell.

Getting to school was no problem, but the teachers would forget to release a volunteer and me early enough, so I'd end up at the final bell with everyone disappearing to catch buses etcetera, except for one boy. Bless his heart. The tiniest, scrawniest kid in class that only just saw over the top of my wheelchair. But each day he got me home.

So here am I in this wheelchair, not the best thing to impress the boys with. However, I gave it a good crack and still tried to play the feminine, flirty card as there was a guy (there's always a guy), who I had a crush on at school.

He dared me to go down the steep ramp in my wheelchair.
So let me try and explain this ramp. Not only was it steep, it ended abruptly in a dogleg. To make matters worse, there was a great big wall running parallel to the dogleg with very little gap to make the turn.

The dare also included … no hands!

Of course, I obliged. He was very cute after all, and heart won over head.

Down the ramp I flew, picking up speed, totally out of control and then it happened. The wheelchair swerved into the side of the ramp, which projected me out of the chair and I was face planted into the concrete of the dogleg, missing the wall by a fraction.

Blood was streaming, I was screaming like a banshee and the boy was saying, "Oh, Stacey, you've lost your tooth!!!"
So, not only was I bloody and crying, I was toothless as well … not a good look to try and impress the love of your life!!!

However, always an upside. The boy gathered me in his arms and carried me carefully to the sickbay. If I hadn't been in so much pain I really would have enjoyed that so much more.

How fast? Showing Off . . . Again!

Seventh form year, we were allowed off the school grounds for school business and as I was on the magazine committee, a couple of other students and I were sent into town to plead for advertising from the local businesses.

One of these students was a guy I fancied (again!), and so, the 'show off' part of me emerged.

Not far from the school was quite a steep descending hill which I decided would be a great place to show off what 'Roche the Rebel' could do.

At the top of the hill I said to the guy, "Check this out" and powered down the hill at top speed. As I approached the turn I jammed on the brakes. This was meant to stop me immediately and show off my bike skills.

No such luck! Little did I know the disc brakes were extremely efficient locking the back wheel up causing the trike to somersault forward. My feet were strapped in hence I was attached to the trike and did the somersault as well.

Again, another face plant, but this time the trike didn't stop there. It then rolled over landing in the gorse bushes on the side of the hill. Prickly stuff is gorse!!!! Trying to get a screaming, bloody Dribbly Wobbly out was beyond his capabilities, so the hot guy hightailed it back to school to get help. The staff that arrived assessed the situation, and they too couldn't get me out, so it was decided to call the ambulance.

Needless to say my attempt at impressing failed miserably, although I did get to ride in an ambulance with a hunky paramedic.

"I Can Make This Work"

This was my dad's catchphrase all throughout my life. Even now, he's always coming up with creative ways I can do stuff. None best illustrates this point than the Rock Hopping adventure.

When I was about twelve my school class went on a very basic 'survival' school camp.

The teachers were concerned that I wouldn't survive without support, therefore, Dad put his hand up to be there for me.

We arrived at a very spartan campsite in the bush and immediately everyone set about putting up their own tents. This, along with cooking our own food, was the criteria. I sort of helped Dad put up our tent, although I was probably more of a hindrance than a help, but Dad went along with it and soon our accommodation for the night was ready.

The next thing was cooking our dinner. Not really advisable for me to be near naked flames, so again, Dad stepped up and made us a yummy feed in the pot hanging over the camp burner.

The next morning, the kids and teachers set off rock hopping down the river to explore. As this was humanly impossible for me, it was decided that Dad and I would stay at base camp. I didn't mind at all, however, Dad had different ideas. "Right, Stace, you are going to rock hop. Jump on my back."

"No, no, Dad, I'm alright I think I'm too heavy for you."

Let me paint you a picture, dear Reader. At this age, I was a skinny little thing and not really heavy at all. Plus, Dad, being an ex-freestyle Olympic wrestler and still in his physical prime, was strong with phenomenal balance and agility.

"C'mon, Stace, we're going to do this."

"Aww ... okay."

Secretly fearing for my life, I climbed onto his back.

"Just relax, I've got you," he said as I circled my arms around his neck and squeezed a bit too tight. A CP thing ... muscles contracting and locking in.

And we were off.

Down the bank to the river. The first few rocks were easy and I was starting to relax a little bit, but I could see ahead of us and the rocks were getting sparse and larger.

 "Isn't this fun, Stace?"

"Yeah, yeah, we can stop now, Dad, you've shown me how rock hopping works so I'm happy and we can stop."

"Nah, we're only getting started, the best bits are yet to come."

To top it off, because my head was right next to Dad's ear, I had to whisper. Whispering for a CP is nigh on impossible, so between nearly choking Dad and deafening him, he couldn't have been having that much fun. He didn't show it though as he nimbly navigated his way over the huge boulders that now surrounded us in the fast-flowing river with a terrified Dribbly Wobbly clamped on his back.

After we got to where we were going, Dad sat me on the biggest rock he could find. I looked back down the river to our campsite and realised just how far we had come. What an amazing adventure Dad had given me and from then on I wasn't scared.

Perhaps it was the nerves or maybe it was the bean stew the night before, but whatever it was I needed a poo.

There is a particular position that CPs can't do – squatting. All the other kids had no problem with this, but for me, it was impossible as I would have just landed in it!!!

Dad came to the rescue again with his catchphrase,
"I've got this."
Before I knew it, he had fashioned a toilet for me out of stones, then he wandered off into the bush to give me some privacy.
Oh, the relief.

Suddenly Dad called out, "Are you finished? Cause the kids are coming back."
Quickly, I pulled my pants up and covered the makeshift loo and by the time I got to Dad, the kids were in our part of the river.
"How did you get here?" one kid asked me. "You can't climb over rocks."
I replied, "I flew here."
I really did because to me, my dad is Superman.

Sailing Away

My last year at secondary school was a really good example of creative thinking by a few teachers.

I wanted to take physical education as a University Entrance subject. This posed quite a few major obstacles as the course was designed for sporty, non-disabled athletes. By now, I had discovered the sport of Boccia (explanation of this later), and had become quite proficient at it, which was what had prompted me to take this particular subject.

When I said I wanted to take PE, the teachers baulked as they could see some major complications for me to achieve the marks needed to pass. But I was adamant.
One of the requirements of the course was to do ten physical exercises relating to athletics. Now, for me, that just wasn't achievable, so approval was given for me to do ten similar exercises around Boccia. This was my foray into adapting and modifying as I tried to keep the activities I had to do as close as I could to what my peer group was doing.

But the biggest hurdle to overcome was the end of year exam that was conducted on the water. The students had to rig, sail and unrig a P-class yacht completely by themselves. Everyone thought this was going to be a real stumbling block for me as it was not only physically impossible but a safety issue as well. You can see the headlines now ...

'Dribbly Wobbly Launches Boat and is Now Halfway to Australia!'

The teachers put their heads together and came up with a solution that really blew us away. I was to give verbal instructions throughout the exam.
Instead of me sailing the P-class, my teacher sourced a catamaran for me to have something safer to be on when out on the water. How awesome of him to have found this yacht and for the owner to let me experience sailing.

We began on the shore and I instructed my teacher exactly how to rig the yacht. I was then put into a meaty, Dribbly Wobbly-proof life jacket and got onto the catamaran, and from there instructed the teacher how to sail the course.
"Tac to Port", "Gybe away", "Don't let the sail luff"

I was pretty proficient at all the lingo during my exam. I got both of us around the course without falling overboard or hitting any buoys (or boys). Then it was to shore and instructing the un-rigging.

I passed with flying colours ... actually could say I sailed through! I felt that I had achieved exactly the same as my peers but just did it in a different way.

Like the cross-country teacher, this teacher had shaped my future into the sporting world and shown me creativity at its best. Who knows if I hadn't experienced this, would I have gone on to have a career in sport or even been a sportsperson?

5.

DISCOVERIES

The Name is Stacey.

"Hi, my name is Stacey."

"Hi, Tracey."

"No, it's Stacey."

"Yes, I said Tracey."

"No, no, Stacey is my name"

"Riiiiight – Trrraaaceeeey"

"Okay … whatever, I'm Tracey."

This has been a conversation I have had all through my life and I'm quite honestly getting tired of it. I even contemplated officially changing my name to Tracey and being done with it. But then I thought, nah, the conversation would probably go:

"Hi, my name is Tracey."

"Hi, Stacey."

"No, it's Tracey."

"Yes, I said Stacey."

"No, no, Tracey is my name"

"Riiiiight – Stttaaaceeeey"

"Okay … Whatever, I'm Stacey."

I talked to Mum about this and asked her why did she name me with such a hard name to pronounce and her reply was,

"We didn't know you were going to have speech difficulties and mess up your name every time."

Have you guessed yet, Reader? There's great humour in our family. This allows me to look at the above and similar situations with laughter.

Knowledge Is Power.

As previously mentioned, we weren't told a heck of a lot about Cerebral Palsy back when I was young. Actually, no one in my family realised the reflexes that spontaneously happened were all part of it. There were a number of things I kept doing that were obviously part of CP we didn't understood why.

So why didn't the doctors tell Mum and Dad about these 'attributes' of CP? I guess they didn't think my parents needed to know. If this is the case … how wrong they were. Also, back in those days, research wasn't prolific and access to it was non-existent.

Where do these spontaneous reflexes come from? Well, Mother Nature has given a newborn infant many innate survival skills. These reflexes can make baby seem like a bundle of nerves with the twitching, jerking and kicking at really odd times, but they are actually necessary and tells us that baby is just fine.

As the baby grows many of these responses disappear because baby doesn't need them anymore.

However, for those with CP one or all of the infant reflexes are retained.

For me, they are the Startle Reflex and the Grasp Reflex (which I call Spaz Grab).

Startle Reflex: This happens when I get a fright. The adrenaline surges, my heart beats faster and my muscles contract. The result is an involuntary jump of my arms extending outwards and upwards (my personal scribbler just asked me what my body does when this happens ... I don't know, I'm the one getting the fright! I suggested to her to give me a fright and video it, but she'd prefer not to research that one).

Put it this way, a lot of wine glasses have been harmed during this event.

I do an exceptional version of the YMCA dance without music and without meaning to. It has got me into a lot of tight spots over the years. Some results cause injuries and some results cause apologies.

Spaz Grab: Not the official title but pretty bang on to what I do. This is slightly different from the Infant Grasp reflex insofar as rather than grip when something is put into my hand; I only grip when I'm under stress and already holding something.

To give an example. I was on a school camp trip and one of the activities was to abseil down a cliff face. Getting up to the top was fine and getting strapped into the harness was fine, the problem came when I went over the side and was about halfway down. Suddenly I lost my balance, fell sideways and ended upside down which totally freaked me out and the Spaz Grab kicked in. For love or money, I would not let go of that rope ... actually, COULDN'T let go of the rope. The instructor called to me "Just release your grasp and we can lower you down easily."

Hahaha, little did they know that the Spaz Grab was in play. I'm pretty sure they thought I was just being a drama queen because they had no option but to pull me back up to the top of the cliff. It was there they discovered my secret power as the instructor prized my hand off the rope.
I had held on so tightly that my fingernails had made indentations into the palm of my hand and the marks remained there for a couple of days.

This is why you need to know that your child with CP will get a fright when you call her name suddenly or tickle her and because of that fright she will have a Startle Reflex and will involuntarily knee you in the face or, because of the Grasp Reflex, she can't let go of her spoon after she's finished eating. All this stuff is pretty vital to be able to understand your child.

And from the child's point of view, it would be nice to understand why she's exhausted when sitting on her Dad's shoulders or why she drops stuff when the door slams shut.

Another part of CP, which is relatively common, is absorbing information at the same rate as classmates. There is no problem with learning the information; it's just absorbed differently. Now, if the child doesn't know that it is part of CP she will assume that there is something else wrong with her in terms of her intellect.

Over the years I developed tools to help me out of different circumstances that are caused by my CP.

For example. If I got into a situation where I was in danger of losing physical control which could result in injury, I would start to sing a few lines of a particular song. This would relax me and allow me to extricate myself out of the tricky situation. It worked every time. I would like to thank Frankie Goes to Hollywood for saving my life on many occasions as I would sing

♪♪♪ *"Relax don't do it if you don't want to die."* ♪♪♪

That last bit I changed for the precarious circumstances I was in.

Dad's Career

If it hadn't been for my dad getting involved in the disability sports sector and learning so much we could all still be in the dark and I would still be blaming myself for the stupid stuff I do instead of the CP.

From humble beginnings, my father started his career as a panel beater, moved on to become a prison officer, then returned to being a panel beater. But because he was always strongly involved with sports (national coach of Olympic wrestling), he gravitated towards the sports sector.

Starting with children's sport in school, he was then introduced to disability sports through an event we went to together.

Rarotonga

From the ages of eight to sixteen years old, I attended an event called The Mini Olympics. This all-weekend event was held for both physically and intellectually disabled children.

Teams were made up from the different regions around the North Island.

This was a 'have a go, everyone gets a gold medal' type of event. However, it was because of these games that I soon developed my competitive edge which I took on into my sporting career.

In my last year when I was sixteen, it was decided to take the event to Rarotonga. Naturally, everyone was excited and Dad put his hand up to be parent help.

What an awesome trip. Dad and I hired a scooter and travelled around the island having fun which raised a few eyebrows. Little did we know (and I still to this day, cringe) that some woman got it into her head to make a complaint that athletes shouldn't be allowed to bring their boyfriends along.

"Ewww!!!! He's my DAD!!!!"

Dad, on the other hand, loves telling that story,

Continuing with Dad's Career.

It was during this event that Dad met some movers and shakers in the disability sports sector, and through this, he was given the opportunity to get involved in the new training course being set up in New Zealand.

The training course was called Coaching Athletes with Disabilities or CAD and it was here that Dad began his quest for knowledge, and specifically around CP. I'm very proud to say that Dad co-wrote a manual and there is a very cute photo of me trying to throw the shot-put in it.

Once this knowledge became accessible it empowered all of us and allowed us to grow our relationship because now, the true characteristics of my CP were understood. This was life-changing for me too because it answered all the questions on why I did the things I did, and I didn't need to berate myself or be ashamed of who I am.

I am an intelligent woman … Knowledge is Power.

Insight into the Human Psyche

I was super excited to join Brownies because my mates had been telling me all about the cool stuff that they were doing.

I easily talked my mum and dad into letting me become a Brownie. They bought me the uniform and I turned up in my brightly coloured turtleneck (a mustard yellow skivvy), with a brown dress over the top just like everyone else.

The first game was where everyone sat in a circle and one ran around the outside in order to tap a girl on the head. She then jumped up and took over the running.

At my very first go, I promptly fell over. The leader freaked out and put me in the middle of the circle. There I had to sit on the toadstool for the rest of the night.

This was a real downer!

I saw something in that leader's eyes, which made me realise she was never going to let me join in any rough games.

Result? I pulled the pin and never went back.

Ironically, I got nothing from Brownies but joined Guides, then Rangers. The difference in leaders was like night and day, and instantly I was accepted and encouraged to participate fully.

I went on to achieve the highest honour in the Guiding fraternity, which is the Queen's Guide award bestowed on me by the N.Z. Governor General. I am very proud of this achievement.

From then I have developed an insight into the human psyche and seem to have a 'sixth sense' (not of seeing dead people) of being able to 'know' whether someone is genuine or just a wanker.

All throughout my life I have experienced people's assumptions of my perceived abilities or lack thereof.

Which reminds me of a quote by Albert Einstein that goes:

> *'Everyone is a genius. But if you judge a fish by its ability to climb a tree, it will live its whole life believing that it is stupid.'*

When I was younger, I always wanted to prove people wrong and make them believe that I could easily accomplish things. Therefore, whenever I could, I'd do some quite crazy stuff … like bungee jumping and tandem skydiving (see the chapter on 'My Crazy Stunts).

However, now that I'm older, I have stopped caring about what people think of me and of trying to prove myself. Mind you, this is a really hard habit to break, and I still catch myself slipping back into the 'proving' mode every so often.

You see …

It's human nature for people to want to make a good first impression, but for me, it's a little more intense. I feel that I have to prove my intelligence to people right off the bat. If they don't pick up that I'm intelligent in the first minute of meeting me, they've gone to the dark side thinking my brain is utter mush. This is an exhausting thing to have to do each time I meet a new person. Now that I'm older, I realise that I'm doing it, but feel that it's the only way I can immediately affect their judgement of me.

When you first meet me, you will hear my crazy voice and see my crazy body movements and this is where you can assume there's nothing between the ears.

If you don't understand what I say, just ask me to repeat it, cause I tell you that there is nothing worse than people pretending they know what I've said ... example:

I ask, "Where is the toilet?"

And get the reply, "Yes, I'm well, thank you."

(I do wonder why they just can't try a little harder to listen.)

This relates not only to me but to anyone you may come across who has a speech difficulty. One of my best mates in the whole wide world is the most intelligent and articulate man I've ever met. Because of his CP, the way he talks is extremely difficult to understand and he always gets written off, which is, sadly, their loss.

I do use humour a lot to deflect any assumptions that people make on my intelligence, which sometimes can get me into trouble. A lot of people don't get my humour as it can be rather dark and self-deprecating. Also, many of them don't expect me to have the intelligence to be witty.

A good example of this is the reaction I would get when I'd tell people the title of this book. I think it sums me up perfectly, but it's almost like others got offended on my behalf.

The term 'Dribbly Wobbly' is something I came up with when I was younger as I do dribble and I do wobble. My family embraced it with all the fun I intended it to have.

Surely the cartoon shows that the front cover is all tongue-in-cheek ... I love it!

I wish I could walk around with my C.V. tattooed on my forehead so people would instantly know that I have a Bachelor of Arts, I had a 'real' job, I own my own home, I drive, I'm on numerous Boards of Trustees, and I have a very full life.

Now the kumbaya part of me thinks I should be myself and let the people make up their own mind ... what a silly thing for me to think. No. I will continue to do the first minute meeting as intelligently and wittily as I can.

Discovering That Cerebral Palsy Wasn't Going Away.

When I was a little girl, I often had a bath with my sister who was there to stop me from drowning. Around this time I was becoming aware of my differences and one night my sister and I got talking.

Now, I really thought I was going to grow out of CP, so in the bath, I asked her, "When am I going to get better?"

The four years between my older sister and me was enough for her to understand that this was a serious question and that I needed not only a serious answer, but I needed her to be honest and straight-up with me.

My sister is very protective of me, but she's also a realist and because of this, she told me straight that I was never going to get better from CP.

I burst into tears and cried for ages as the hope drained from my body just as the water drained out of the bath that night. It sounds like my sister was very harsh, but on the contrary, she actually showed me so much love by telling me the truth.

It's always hard to learn a truth especially one as dramatic as that, but when it's told by someone you love and who you know loves you, it makes it seem more bearable. She was quite right in telling me that night as I look back and see that it was a monumental shift in my perception of myself and propelled me forward into my reality which I could then deal with.

CP was here to stay for better or for worse. There was a lot of 'worse' but happily, there has been a lot of 'better' as well.

My First Role Model

I have a lot of role models that I look up to and get inspiration from, but Lisa Vassal author of *'Just an Ordinary Kid'* was my very first.

On a family trip, we happened to stay at Lisa's parents' motel, and when I got out of the car, they recognized a fellow CP.

That's right – Lisa has CP just like me.

Now, I never actually met Lisa but I did speak to her on the phone to thank her for sending me her book after her parents had told her about me.

As a child, I'd never read any stories about someone like me. Back in those days there just weren't any around, so for me to come across Lisa's book was a revelation.

Reading that book allowed me to understand that what I thought about myself was not dissimilar to how Lisa thought of herself in the same situation.

Lisa's book is still with me to this day, and I have read it many times as it continues to be my touchstone.

And while on the subject of inspiration, I feel a little rant coming on.

It's sad that I've got to a point where I can't take compliments very well as I don't know if they are genuine or if they come from a place of condescension. Throughout my life, people have told me that I inspire them, I always ask why ... is it because I'm a Dribbly Wobbly that gets out of bed every morning and gets dressed, or is it because I've done something pretty good? The two have blurred for me and I really struggle knowing when to accept and enjoy the compliment and when to know it's just a platitude.

Because I portray myself as a strong, independent woman, people sometimes don't understand my struggle. On the one hand, I pride myself on portraying this strong image, but on the other hand, there are times when I do wish that people could see what I deal with twenty-four seven. For example; falling over randomly, then having to get up and go out to meet people who expect me to be on my game.

This is why Lisa's story resonated with me and still does to this day. She grappled with the same issues and showed me how to overcome them . . .

Mic drop   

6.

MY CRAZY STUNTS

I always knew I was different, so to overcome this said difference, I periodically felt the need to prove myself to others. In order to satisfy this need, I really did do some quite crazy stunts.

Let's start with:

Bungee Jumping

My dad and brother had been on a wrestling trip down south, and on their way back, they stopped in Taupo for the night. There they decided they would go and do a bungee jump. This was in 1992, and it was still quite a new commercial venture.

When they got home, they were really buzzing about their adventure, and from then on, I wanted the experience too.

It was eighty dollars which was quite a lot for a fourteen-year-old, but I saved and managed to get it all.

My parents and grandparents were going to Taupo for a golfing trip and so this was an opportune time for me to do the bungee jump.

After discussing Dad's first experience where he said that his top had flown up over his head, Mum proceeded to pin my jersey to my undies as she tucked it into my trousers. I looked like a right nerd, but it was a necessary evil.

We arrived at the designated spot, which was a unique cantilever platform projecting out from the cliff-top forty-seven metres above the waters of the Waikato River.

There was one person ahead of us, a guy in his twenties with his girlfriend watching on. The poor guy stood on the edge for twenty minutes before he admitted defeat and backed away from the edge much to his girlfriend's bemusement.

My turn.
Strapped in, heavy bungee rope around my ankles and the instructor holding on tight so I wouldn't fall off unexpectedly, I stepped forward to the edge.

"3 .... 2 .... 1 .... BUNGEE," the man yelled.
Stupidly I took a look down ... "OMG!! It's a long way down."

I glanced at the guy who was being consoled by his girlfriend, and I knew I had to do it and not wuss out like he had. So I told the instructor to count me down again.
"3 .... 2 .... 1 .... BUNGEE."

This time I went!

My technique wasn't the recommended fall. You're supposed to go in a graceful gliding motion. Me? Graceful? No, no, I just stepped out off the platform, which meant I went feet first. Then, as the bungee rope took over, it violently flung me around so I was facing the way I was supposed to = facing the water. Even though the propulsion was violent, it didn't hurt at all and was just a major adrenaline rush.

Dad then did his jump and we met in the boat below. Comrades, with a new-found bond between father and daughter.

We went back to the office and the staff were so happy and full of admiration (this was a time that the admiration was definitely genuine), that they gave me the T-shirt and the video of my jump as a gift. The reason? I was the first disabled person to have done a bungee jump in Taupo.

In the debrief with Mum and grandparents, I learned that the girlfriend of the guy that had chickened out said to him, "How do you feel now?" just as I left the platform.
Would I do it again? No!

Tandem Skydiving

Now I'm seventeen years old. The glory of the bungee jump had definitely worn off, and I felt like I needed to do another crazy stunt to prove my prowess.

This time, I selected a tandem skydive. It was more expensive and so it took me longer to save up for, but when I got there it was all the sweeter.

My grandparents took me to the airfield where I met the pretty handsome instructor I was soon to be strapped to. As a teenager, this was an added bonus.

There was no hoo-hah with instructing me on what I was to do. It's not rocket science, and as I look back, I really appreciated that the instructor showed no fuss and treated me as just another customer.

Cut to the plane.

Last-minute instructions given, goggles put on and then we're moving to the door. It opens and it literally takes my breath away ... like really, I couldn't breathe.
"Look at the camera on the wing," he called before leaping out the door. Needless to say, the image is of a stunned mullet.

The breath finally came back when he pulled the cord. However, so did a shot of pain as the harness around my thighs was too tight and the jolt made it even tighter.
Because of the pain I was in, I didn't fully enjoy the ride down, but as soon as we landed, the pain dissipated and the ecstasy of the jump overwhelmed me.

As a bonus for me, they decided we would land on the Mount beach. This is a beautiful beach that is crowded during summer but in the early spring when I did the jump, it should have been relatively deserted.

It wasn't.

Unbeknown to the skydiving people, there was a funeral going on exactly where we had to land. Imagine the horror of those attending the funeral when they got gatecrashed by me screaming on landing and noisily disturbing the peaceful proceedings.

Would I do it again? No!

Paragliding

I can't remember exactly how this came about, but I know it was part of my whole 'prove to the world' thing and so it just was something I had to do.

The day that we had booked wasn't exactly the ideal weather conditions, however, because I had travelled a bit of a distance, it was decided that we'd do it anyway.

We arrived and, we were driven to the top of the small mountain where lift-off was to take place.

I was safely strapped onto the instructor, and with everything checked we (well, he), ran off the side of the mountain to get airborne.

Now, the normal method is to glide majestically off and out over the vista below.

However, this is me we're talking about, although my excuse is that the weather was against us.

No gliding … 'plummeting' would be a more accurate term to use as we headed downward at a rather fast rate and crashed into the bushes below.

Neither of us was injured as the guy had done extremely well with the abortive landing. However, we were stuck there until the cavalry arrived to haul us out. I didn't mind too much as I certainly had had fun.

Would I do it again … Maybe, if the weather conditions were right.

White-Water Rafting on Kaituna River

In my late teens, I was given the opportunity to attend a regional sports camp for disabled youth, which was held in an area renowned for adventures.

It was a week of full-on action and surprisingly I got in with the cool crowd. Most of these kids were the helpers and were non-disabled people. Naturally, I honed in on the cutest guy (the other crip in the cool crowd), and developed a crush on him.
The activities included a rope course, abseiling and the usual team-building exercises.

In the evenings, there was storytelling around the campfire, games with torches, and other fun things.

It was an extremely great fun-filled camp.

Then …

I made a stupid decision to go on the white-water rafting adventure, which, unbeknown to me, was a Grade 5 river, which is the hardest of the lot.

Life jackets on, instructions given (although I didn't equate these instructions to actual death), and into the inflatable raft. My only job was to hang on and not fall out. I thought this would be pretty simple and settled in for the fun.

OMG!!! We hit the first of many Grade 5 furious rapids … I'M NOT IN KANSAS ANYMORE!

From then on, for two-and-a half-hours, I was literally afraid for my life. I hung on for grim death, knuckles white, teeth clenched, brain in overdrive. Was I going to make it?
All this was before the health and safety law got really pedantic … I mean, who in their right mind would put a whole lot of crips in a rubber boat and chuck them down a scary river at speed???

But I made it.

Would I do it again? No, No, No!

Back at the camp, on terra firma, the fun started again.

The last night was epic! We went out to a fancy restaurant. Now, I had not prepared for this event, so I only had my track pants packed. Never fear; the cool kids dressed me in their clothes from shoes, to dress, to coat. I looked fabulous.

After the dinner, we bribed one of the older instructors to smuggle some alcohol back into the camp. As everyone went to bed, we took over the common room and proceeded to party all night.

The party was that good that it comes as no surprise I made a move on my crush. My first 'real' kiss, although I can't really say that because as soon as we locked lips, I started laughing hysterically and that blew the mood.

My first kiss, and I can't even remember his name.

This camp was more than just that week. It had a few repercussions that I didn't discover until many years later.

Repercussions From the Camp

First Kiss

This was a real blast from the past.

Fast forward seven years from the above-mentioned camp.

I went with my sister to her friend's hen party, which was a pub crawl all around the Waikato. One of the pubs that we stopped off at, I noticed a guy sitting in the corner and thought he looked familiar.

As we walked closer, he recognised me and came over to say hi. Oh my goodness, he was my 'first kiss' guy.

By this time in the hen journey, enough alcohol had been consumed, so everyone wanted to know who this guy was and I was more than happy to announce to the whole bar that he was my 'First Kiss'.

The guy shrank back into the corner and stayed there. Fine by me because I'd had beer goggles on that night when we'd kissed. Now, my standards had risen, and I didn't find anything attractive at all about him.

Thankfully the hen party bus arrived and we were off to our next destination.

Ringo

A photo album is such a memory jerker. My partner at the time, Ringo, and I were living together, and I was telling the story about a camp I'd been on using the photos as props.

Imagine my surprise when he pointed to one of the guys in the group shot and said, "That's me."

It turns out Ringo had been on the same camp. Oh, how I had so many good memories from that camp … but … none of him. In fact, once pointed out, I remembered that he had been a complete weirdo, and I had avoided him that whole week.

Talk about stuff coming back at you.

I should have heeded my own instinct and stayed clear. Ringo and I parted company not long after that.

I've Got This

My older and much wiser, cultured, rad sister was at university in Dunedin, a South Island city very famous for student parties and raucous behaviour. So, of course, I was super stoked when she invited me to spend a week with her and, being fifteen years old, this trip was my first adventure without Mum and Dad.

Although the student parties and raucous behaviour were not quite my sister's style, I did have some really 'student' experiences that made me feel extremely grown up and part of her crowd.

Her flat was awesome. Okay it was cold, old, damp, and with really dilapidated furniture, which was all the cool stuff that students have, so I was in heaven. Her flatmates and friends were all super lovely and embraced me into their world.

A Cold Noddy

Halfway through the week, I saw a few people with really, really short hair, and to top it off, my favourite band, The Cranberries' lead singer had also shaved her hair off.

That was for me. My sister took me to a really funky hairdresser and I told her what I wanted. The clippers came out, and within minutes, all my hair was on the floor. What was I thinking??? It was the middle of winter in the South Island, freezing cold conditions and I go and shave my head. And to top it off, I have a really ugly head when bald.

The moment I looked in the mirror, I decided I needed to grow my hair again. The beanie came out and didn't come off.

Chair Lift of Death

A carload of uni students with me in tow, headed off further south to the adventure capital of New Zealand, Queenstown. This was the first time I'd been there so it was simply a done deal that I was shown all the sights.

One of these was the famous Coronet Peak ski fields.

Now, I had seen snow a couple of times before, but I really wanted to get up the mountain and get amongst the snow bunnies and ski instructors.

I talked my sister into going up on the chairlift to the top. She was a bit nervous as it was going to be quite an ordeal for me to get on and off. However, she relented and off we went.

If you've never seen a chairlift before then let me explain how they work. They go around in a circle, slowing down slightly for the getting on and off process. This is fine for those who have skis and good balance, but for those of us who don't have their balance under control, it just may pose a slight problem.

The chairlift operator dutifully helped me on as my sister got on the other side. Easy. Both of us enjoyed the ride up taking in the massive, breath-taking scenery.

At the top, we got off without a hitch and stayed long enough to have a bit of a play in the snow. However, I soon discovered that walking in the snow was not as easy as it looked.

It was then time to head down the mountain.

Easy ... We've got this.

We got into position, but just as the chair came around, I stumbled. My sister grabbed me and got me safely onto the chair, but she didn't have time to get on herself.

PANIC!!!

Well, not for me. Surprisingly, I was quite calm. My sister, on the other hand, was calling out to stop the lift, something that couldn't be done, so she jumped on the chair behind and started calling instructions to me including for me to STAY STILL.

'Stay still' is not really the best thing for me to hear in any circumstance, as my natural body reaction to that command is to do the complete opposite.

It was apparent to her that the safety bar had not come down meaning I wasn't locked in, and she was terrified that I'd fall.

As the chairlift left the platform, it quickly dropped over the side of the mountain where I saw nothing but space and potential death. I grappled with the bar that was over my head and tried to pull it down. It was extremely heavy, and it just didn't want to go without a fight. Now I was getting a bit worried. There was nothing to prevent me from plummeting down a long way to my death.

After quite a few jiggles and wiggles with the bar, which caused the whole chair to swing almost out of control, it gave in, came down, and locked into place. I could hear my sister breathe a sigh of relief.

The rest of the descent was fine, but we still had to tackle me getting off the beast. The guy at the top had radioed down to the operator warning that there was a Dribbly Wobbly on the way who was certainly going to need assistance.
What is it about ski operators and instructors? They're always good looking! And this guy was no different.
So, I was quite happy to jump into his arms as he pulled up the bar, steadied the chair, and physically helped me off. Didn't last long enough!

My sister arrived soon after and was relieved that the whole thing was over and I had survived.
Drinks all round and another story to tell!
Would I do it again? Of course! But I don't think my sister would.

7.

BOCCIA

As I mentioned earlier, I come from a very sporty family. In my youth, sport was everywhere and everything, and because I was mainstreamed, I participated in mainstream sport. As time went on, the gap between my peers and myself widened which made me realise I couldn't excel.

I tried many different sports which produced some pretty average results but my dad always encouraged me to never give up.

The first sport I tried in view of being competitive was swimming.

Dad found a mainstream swimming coach for me and she came all the way out to our country public warm pools where I would just flail around for an hour. Even though she would 'try' to teach me the techniques of swimming, I'm sure her main role was to actually just prevent me from drowning.

Consequently, swimming was canned.

Next!

Shot Put and Discus – or, in my words, Shot Put and The Flat Thing, as for the life of me, I could never remember the word 'discus'. So to this day, people hassle me about throwing the Shot Put and the Flat Thing.

This was a success. Well, on the record books anyway. I was the N.Z. record holder for my age group in my classification. Now this does sound flash, doesn't it? However, you need to know that I was the only one in my classification for Shot Put and the Flat Thing in N.Z.!

Visualise this …

The Shot Put and Discus area is full of very serious, muscly, and athletic men and women from the different classification in disability sport.

A competitor steps forward into the throwing circle. A hush descends over the crowd, and the expectation is palpable. The officials are out around twelve metres away, preparing to measure the powerful throw. An elongated grunt comes from the athlete as he releases the shot put. The crowd cheer and the officials extend the tape even further.

My name is called. I step into the circle. Immediately the tape measure is wound up as the officials jog in to wait just in front of me.

Good visualising!!!

My record breaker was around one and a half metres ... a tad different to the other competitors.

My biggest challenge was to not FALL out of the circle and thus be disqualified, an accomplishment almost as great as the actual throw. I should have got a gold medal just for that.

A metre and a half in anyone's language is rubbish even if you're the record holder, so thank goodness, boccia came along when it did.

Let me introduce this great sport of boccia. It has its origins in Italy from the game of bocce and is a cross between indoor bowls and pétanque played with leather balls in an indoor setting.

Originally designed for people with significant cerebral palsy who must be in a wheelchair to play.

My dad was over in Australia for work in 1995 and saw this sport being played only by ramp players (these are players who use a ramp to propel the ball).

He came back to N.Z. and the next thing he'd got a couple of guys ready for the World Champs in Australia.

It was at these games Dad discovered that a player didn't need a ramp at all to play this sport and he met a sportswoman who reminded him so much of me that he thought this could be the ideal sport that I was searching for.

Through this discovery, Dad transferred his coaching knowledge from wrestling to boccia, and he became the national boccia coach. I took to it like a duck to water and was instantly successful. This was 199. By 2000, I was ready for the Paralympics being held in Sydney.

Let me backtrack.

1996 – Australian National Championship

My first international tournament and, although an Australian national championship, it was extended to New Zealand players.

This was where I met George, an Australian boccia player, who went on to annihilate me in all our matches of that tournament. It was a hard lesson to have to learn in my first international, but I was adamant this would never happen again. When I got home, I went back to the drawing board and devised strategies that served me well in future tournaments.

1997 – Asia-Pacific Championship

The following year was the Asia-Pacific champs. By now I had learnt how to play the game, literally and figuratively.

George and I got into the finals, but to his disadvantage, I'd figured out that he had a crush on me. This was my weapon and I used it beautifully to my advantage.

The tables had turned from the year before, and now it was me in the winning seat.

This was my first major success ... achievement ... accomplishment ... glory ... taste of victory in my life and I was hooked.

Two Blinkies and a Weightlifter.

After my victory, a celebration was in order.

Because it was the Asia-Pacific championships it was a multi-sport tournament, so at the end there was a large awards dinner where all of the athletes from all the codes got together.

Around the table I was at, there were two 'Blinkies' (visual impairment), a weightlifter and a swimmer. After dinner the swimmer disappeared which left just the four of us in good conversation.

The wine at the table had been supplied so none of us hesitated as we had accomplished our goals and wanted to celebrate.

The weightlifter and I decided to head off to another bar, but I soon got bored and decided to go and find the Blinkies.

After a bit of searching, I found out that they had gone to the spa, thought that was a great idea and wandered off. Sure enough, I found the two Blinkies soaking in the hot tub.

It didn't take me long to discover that those Blinkies turned out to be as boring as the weightlifter, so I carefully removed myself from the spa without their knowledge and made a quiet exit while they were still chatting to me. That in itself was a major accomplishment for a Dribbly Wobbly, but I successfully achieved it, got to my room, and went to sleep.

And oh by the way, I did actually win the Referees' Choice for Best and Fairest Award, and the glass plaque I received journeyed around with me the whole night without getting broken.

1998 World Champs – New York, the Team Got 8th Place.

These championships were held at the Hofstra University in Long Island, New York. It was the biggest sporting event that I'd ever seen or participated in to that date. The level of competition was at a phenomenally high standard, and by the end of it, I had learnt how to conduct myself on a world stage as well as realising that I could foot it with the big boys.

Blowing in the Wind

Being my first 'world' event and being in the N.Z. team, it was very overwhelming especially once I was on the court.
Our first game, unfortunately, was against the World Champions, Korea, so that in itself was a daunting prospect.
Their technique was unorthodox and one I'd never seen before. They sat facing the court, however, they looked back over their shoulder whilst swinging the ball. And the swing … it seemed to take forever to release.

Let me set the scene.

As a player is throwing their ball there must be quiet on the court, and the opposition cannot speak or make a noise otherwise they will be penalised.

The first Korean competitor positioned himself facing the court. Turned his head to look over his shoulder, then proceeded to swing his arm. During the process, he let rip a mighty, lengthy fart.

Remember ... everything is quiet!!!!!

The fart resounded around the massive arena like a drum roll from a Rolling Stones concert. So impressive was this blow of wind that it took us all by surprise.
The Korean team did not bat an eyelid and kept their serious composure intact.

But within two seconds of this mighty gaseous roar, we Kiwis proceeded to hysterically lose the plot. We attempted to do this as quietly as we possibly could, as we didn't want to be penalised. Hell's teeth, the score was already around 15 - nil to the Koreans, we didn't see the need to make it worse.

The fart did wonders for my confidence in the pressure cooker environment I had found myself in and the suppressed laughter we had is something we still delightfully share to this day.

Holding On

It was the middle of summer in New York and the arena was incredibly hot.

While waiting for the next game, I stupidly didn't drink for some time and became slightly dehydrated. Enough so that the coach told me to go upstairs into the cool, air-conditioned first-aid room.

Up there, I was plied with water ... lots of water!

Feeling better, I re-joined the team and we then were called onto the court for our next game. We were up against the home team, U.S.A., who had a massive cheering crowd, which was incredibly annoying as they yelled,
"U-S-A ... U-S-A ... U-S-A."
They did this throughout the match whenever they were allowed to make noise.
I want you to know, Reader, that each game takes around an hour to complete and competitors may not leave the court during this time.

About halfway through the match my rehydrating method kicked in, and the bladder filled up enough to be uncomfortable.
Within ten minutes it was unbearable.

Dad, our coach, seeing me jigging in my chair, called a timeout to talk to me about my distress. As I was not able to leave the court, his advice was that my only option, if it got too much, was to pee myself. OMG – my first international tournament and I would be known as the chick from N.Z. who wet herself on court ... NO WAY!!!!

To makes matters worse, the game went into a tiebreak, which means, as the score is tied after six ends, an extra end is played. Another twenty minutes at least!!!!

By this time, I'm not only rocking, I'm butt clenched, wriggling, legs crossed tightly, and praying to the Peeing Gods that the bladder will hold.

I have no recollection of the rest of that game, as my focus was solely on keeping my dignity intact.

After the final ball was bowled, the team assistant grabbed my chair, and we could have easily broken the 100-metre sprint record getting off the court and into the toilets.

The relief was immense!!!

The New York Subway.

We had a day off and decided to go into the city to discover what New York had to offer.

We took the subway but soon realised that not all stops were created equal. Many didn't provide lifts to get up to street level. And those that did have lifts, well they were used by the homeless as urinals. Consequently, the wheels on our chairs became quite disgusting, and as I was physically pushing my chair, my hands were a mess.

However, this was not the worst thing that happened on this eventful day.

The underground was really quite an amazing place. There were buskers, some of whom were excellent, the graffiti on the walls should have been in galleries, and the crowds were huge rushing to catch their trains or to leave the platform.
Trouble was, we got down into the subway and couldn't seem to find our way out. You see, the goal was to go to the Statue of Liberty, the problem was, we were underneath her but for love or money we couldn't seem to find the lift to get out of there.
For two and a half hours we were roaming around the underground trying to get back up to the fresh air and sky.
We ended up having to go back to where we had started from, but, wow, it was so good when we finally hit the pavement.

1999 World Cup – Argentina, the Team Got 6th Place

All games were straightforward … my bladder held perfectly, there was no untoward barracking crowd, and no one, sadly, farted on court to give us some entertainment.
There was one thing though. This was the first and only time I was close to being penalised for a line or any violation.

In the rules of boccia, you have a four-sided area marked on the floor that your chair and all body parts must remain in.

My technique was to position myself as close to the front line as possible to maximize the full advantage. This time I had got a bit too close and one wheel was actually on the line.

Dad, our coach, was at the other end of the court, saw what I'd done and started coughing to try and alert me to the problem as there was to be silence on court so he couldn't say anything. However, I was in the zone. He was told to stop and so I was totally unaware of my indiscretion.

I had started my shot routine and was about to release the ball when out of the corner of my eye I saw the referee start a step to intercept. Seeing that movement alerted me to something being seriously wrong as it is very unusual for a referee to move an inch when a player is about to deliver the ball.

I stopped. I sat up in my chair and looked down. I was horrified to see that my wheel was on the line. The realisation that I was moments away from being penalised and messing up the whole game sunk in and my heart started to race. How could I have let this happen? I prided myself on ensuring accuracy, I had never been penalised for a line violation ever, and I didn't want to start now. Keeping a poker face, I readjusted my position, started my shot routine again and played the ball.

After that indiscretion, I was paranoid about always checking where my wheelchair was in relation to the box.

The hospitality in Argentina was amazing, and the people were phenomenal hosts which made for an outstanding tournament.

The friendliness continued on to the last night and what a party it was.
One thing I remember vividly happened on the way back to our hotel.
We got off the bus, Dad was pushing one of my teammates and one of the other assistants was pushing me. Naturally, a race ensued.

Luckily for me, Dad and the other guy won because right at the end they didn't take into consideration the couple of steps going down into the hotel lobby.

Dad's reaction was to jam on all brakes, which in turn, propelled my teammate out of his chair and over the steps where he landed on his knees and proceeded to skid along the shiny surface of the foyer.

His entire delivery was so perfect he would have got all tens from the ice-skating judges!

The C.P.'s Version of a Mexican Wave

It was dinnertime; all the athletes from all around the world had gathered in the massive dining room and were partaking of their evening meal.

One of the kitchen hands pushed a trolley full of cutlery out into the dining area.

And then – it happened.

Wait … Let me refresh your memory from Chapter Five explaining the Startle Reflex. You go 'Boo' and I jump. It's a real curse, especially around Guy Fawkes night … but that's another story for another book.

Back to the dining room.

Somehow the cart crashed! And with that, an almighty clang reverberated around the dining room.

One by one the Startle Reflex kicked in as each athlete heard the noise. There was chaos everywhere. Plates went flying, food was propelled onto walls and floor and even up noses. But the best was the 'Mexican Wave' as limbs shot up and out in all directions in a choreographed movement as it flowed around the room.

I didn't appreciate the art form as I was one of the participants, but Dad, who was sitting still, observed the theatrics and said it was one of the funniest moments of chaos he'd ever witnessed.

Thank goodness I didn't have to clean up!

2000 – Qualification Trials for Paralympics Boccia Team

To qualify for the N.Z. Paralympics Boccia team, each member of the team needed to have a finish in the top two of three qualifying tournaments.

In the very last one I was in, Nanny, my paternal grandmother, was in the late stages of bowel cancer.

As soon as my part in the tournament ended, we immediately headed for the airport to catch the late flight home. At check-in, Dad asked if there was an earlier flight and gave the reason why. It was then that he told me she wasn't expected to make it through the night and it was at that moment hearing his voice that I realised the sacrifice he'd made for me.

My immediate reaction was one of guilt. To think that my dad would not see his mother alive again was heart-wrenching and knowing that he had done this for me was awe-inspiring and makes me tear up even now.

My focus had been solely on my goal of being selected in the Paralympics team, and he had my best interests at heart over his own personal situation.

I never really fully articulated my gratitude to him for the sacrifice he made and the way he was able to shelter me from reality over that time. He knew that if I knew the severity of Nanny's illness, I would not have been able to give my best to this important tournament.

I better add here that Dad did get the earlier flight and was able to spend a couple of days with his mother to say goodbye, and so did I.

Nanny would have been so proud to know that, I was not only selected for the N.Z. team, but I was named Captain. I was also the only female and to top it off, the youngest member by about ten years.

2000 Warm-up Paralympics – Korea

Because of our previous performances at the World Cup and the World Champs, we were touted as medal prospects for the upcoming Paralympics, therefore funding was allocated to our team for specialised training camps as all of the team members were scattered throughout New Zealand and needed to be centralised.

As a build-up to the Paras, we had been invited by the South Korean boccia team to visit them in their country and take part in a training camp. Because they were the World Champions at the time, we jumped at the opportunity to learn from the best.

On arrival, we quickly discovered why they were the best. They lived, breathed, ate, slept and trained all together in the one boccia institution.

And when I say 'institution', that's exactly what I mean. The building was grey on the outside and so was its energy. On the inside it was brown … everywhere.

The athletes themselves were very skinny, and we decided that it was because they couldn't get enough to eat. You see, we joined them for lunch one day and were horrified to watch the poor guys try and feed themselves.

They used chopsticks, which for a non-disabled Korean, would not be a problem, but try adding in tremors and you've got a chopstick catastrophe. As the food got closer to the mouth, the more the tremors happened, the less food was left on the chopsticks. I just wanted to go up to them with a spoon and start feeding them myself.

On the first night, we went off to a traditional Korean restaurant where we partook of the local cuisine. It was beautiful on the way down and all seemed well.

Then back in the hotel bathroom things took a turn for the worst. My stomach decided that it didn't like this foreign matter, and I spent the next few hours violently expunging it from my body.

I have never before or since had such projectile vomiting happening. It looked like one of the scenes out of *'The Exorcist'*.

How none of the others in the group didn't get sick defies belief.

Needless to say, the rest of the time the food was from McDonald's.

2000 Paralympics – Sydney. Spoiler Alert, 4th Place

Okay Reader, this is a chapter all in itself so it will follow on in the next couple of pages, I just wanted to put it in so I didn't mess up the chronological order.

2002 World Championship – Portugal, 8th Place
Not A Good Look!

In 2001, I graduated from university and so began my working career. This put huge pressure on my ability to train and maintain the dedication needed for an elite athlete. Consequently, this was the last major tournament for me, and I spent a great deal of time on the sideline.

Portugal itself we could see would have been a majestic and luxurious country in its heyday. However, by the time we arrived, it was sadly run-down, the buildings needed love and even the infrastructure was in disrepair.

The N.Z. team just didn't gel on court and we suffered a humiliating defeat coming 8th after our high of the Paralympics.

The people, however, were wonderful. Like the Argentineans, they were amazing hosts and took pride in providing us with incredible hospitality.

Portugal was my boccia swan song.

8.

2000 PARALYMPICS – SYDNEY

Let's start with a bit of education. What do you think the Paralympics mean? If you answered that they are Olympics for paraplegics you are in the majority of the world population. It is an obvious mistake to make because of the assumption that 'para' is for paraplegic.

The concept was started after WWII for the veterans and civilians who had been injured during the war and around the late 80's the Paralympic movement, as we know it today, was born. The word Paralympic derives from the Greek preposition para meaning beside or alongside.

This means that the Paralympics runs parallel to the Olympics and is equal in the level of competition and recognition (supposedly).

Training Hard

In any elite sport, there is a massive 'behind the scenes' commitment, hours of sheer determination and drive, as well as personal sacrifice. For me, the stress of training, both physically and mentally, was much more intense than I ever imagined it would be. But that's what happens when you strive to be the best.

I was brought up in an environment that if you want to succeed at something, you have to commit to working really hard at it. With the Paralympics on the horizon, the hard work, passion, and drive turned into an obsession. It was all consuming.

As I was still in university at the time, my life involved lectures, study, and training. However, the balance soon shifted, and the focus became more on the training to the point that I felt guilty whenever I wasn't throwing a boccia ball.

The rec centre was on the way to lectures so I was able to persuade my uni mates into taking me there – my wheelchair, my boccia balls, and me. It was all I needed.

I would stay for hours and hours throwing balls, picking up balls, throwing balls, long ends, short ends, driving, drawing, and even trying to perfect a shot of lobbing a ball over the top of another ball (although it never came off during game time).

It was lonely, it was cold, and it was hard. It was a love/hate relationship I formed with that rec centre, but I knew that the work had to be done, and I was the only one who could do it. *'I'm going to the Paralympics! I have to be great, good won't do'.* That thought was relentless and was my only driver, which put me into a tunnel vision, an absorbing modus operandi that made me push myself even more.

Now, I'm sure this story is exactly the same as any athlete who wants to be at the top of his/her game, so I know I'm no different. But I was never told about the feelings that I would have, the biggest one being guilt. That emotion became such a part of my thought pattern. My stomach would churn if I wasn't training. I couldn't think of anything else, even when I had finished a three-hour session. The damn guilt just wouldn't go away.

It was hard not having a coach with me all the time. Dad did his best, but he was not only working full-time, he also lived in a different region. Remember, Reader, back in 2000, the Paralympics were not as supported as they are now. Everyone had full-time study or job, and the team members were scattered around the country.

'Practice makes perfect' – *buzzzzzz* – wrong! PERFECT practice makes perfect!!! This became apparent when I had spent weeks training a certain way on my own. Dad arrived to spend the day with me and check out my training. That's when he saw a bad habit I had picked up. Gutted, to put it mildly, was how I felt. Now I had to go back to Plan A when I was already at Plan W. I picked myself up and dusted myself off and did what I had to do. I was adamant that I was going to be prepared.

Getting Inked

Being in the Paralympics was the biggest, most audacious thing I had ever done and it definitely warranted a symbolic life-long gesture … A TATTOO.

Now, I knew that this was going to be a painful experience, so like a good Girl Guide, I was prepared.

I coerced four of my fellow uni students to come with me. The design? Simple – the Olympic rings.

Considering I was competing on the Paralympics stage – why didn't I get that logo? Well, Reader, do you know what it looks like? It's not a logo that is instantly recognisable, whereas, the Olympic rings are a universal symbol.

Which one do you recognise?

In the tattoo studio, each of the coerced friends had their role. One held my foot down, one held my knee down, one laid across my torso, and one held my hand for comfort. Everyone was given strict instructions to hold tight and not let go. I didn't want my Olympic rings to become Olympic triangles.

To this day, I'm so proud of my tattoo. It says it all and has the bonus of being a great conversation starter.

For example: I was at an airport flying back home from a work trip when a random dude saw my tat. He asked, "Can you tell me what that's about?"

We then had a half hour conversation; one that wouldn't have happened otherwise.

Mind you, there are some idiots out there who will ask me, "So, you like watching the Olympics do you?"

My reply is always, "Yeah, mate, I got a tattoo burnt into my flesh because I like watching the Olympics. Did it not occur to you that I actually represented my country?"

Oh, To Stand Out from the Crowd

Along with the tattoo, I decided I wanted to stamp my individuality onto these games and stand out from the other athletes.

Braids … What says 'individuality' better than a head full of braids!!!! That, with the tat, oh, I was one cool chick.

I found a place – you know a proper Rasta, Bob Marley, 'Ya, mun' type of hair salon and got set to get braided up. Appointment made, a couple of friends – I was doin' it.

Eight hours later!!!!!

I had the slowest braider in the world. I swear that there were around twenty other clients who came and went and I was still in the chair. And it's not like I had long, thick hair.

But the hair did look good until …

A few days after I got back from the games, my sister arrived home from the U.K. for a visit. Once I had shown off 'The Braids', it was time to take them out.

It didn't go as planned.

We soon discovered that the glue used was definitely intended to stick fast to the hair. We eventually got the braids out – but wait, there's more. After washing, the hair matted so much that I could have slipped unnoticed into Bob Marley's following without incident … dreadlocks!!!!

It was time for the hairdresser – a different one. Needless to say, I came out with a lot shorter hair than I had gone in with.

Karma Comes Back and Bites

Cast your mind back, dear Reader, to a previous story of a camp trip I went on to Rotorua and the party on the last night.

To start the team bonding for the Paralympics, all the athletes from the different codes were put together for the first time on the bus ride to Auckland airport.
I heard, from the back of the bus, my name, "Hey, Stacey" yelled down the aisle.
Imagine my surprise when I discovered that the voice belonged to the supervisor of the Rotorua camp Memories came flooding back.

Of course, we had to sit together and reminisce.

He told me how much grief I'd caused him on that camp. It was the first and last camp he'd ever supervised as he got into so much trouble for letting us bring in the alcohol and allowing the party to happen. All I could do was apologise and have a bit of a giggle on how much fun that camp was (except for the white-water rafting).

Funny how your past actions can reverberate through the years and surface at a pinnacle moment to bring memories of such fun days.

At the Games
The Most Magic Moment – The Opening Ceremony

I didn't know what to expect prior to the opening ceremony of the 2000 Sydney Paralympics.

I knew it would be big, but I didn't know just how big.

I knew it would be enjoyable, but I didn't know it would also be so emotional.

I knew it would be a celebration but never in my wildest dreams imagined it to have such an impact on my whole psyche.

The N.Z. Team was waiting our turn to enter the Sydney Olympic Park stadium when our chef de mission spontaneously started a haka, which made me suddenly aware of the enormity of the occasion. I literally felt like I was going to burst with pride.

For those who are unaware of what a haka is, it is a Māori war dance. It was traditionally used on the battlefield, a fierce display of a tribe's pride, strength, and unity.

Being part of this haka and the occasion made the hairs on the back of my neck stand up, it has that much power and mana. The haka cemented our team spirit.

As the haka finished, it was our turn to enter the stadium. We then began the march out from the tunnel and the cheer of the crowd of over 100,000 was deafening. The cheering was for us … our N.Z. team.

I was in my manual wheelchair and I had asked Dad to be by my side for this experience, so although he was pushing my chair he was doing it one-handed. This meant we were walking side by side which symbolised our relationship. It was quite poetic as it emphasised this massive journey that we had undertaken together.

As we got completely into the stadium, we felt the rush of electric energy coming from the crowd and the other athletes. It was palpable and awe-inspiring. It was an emotionally-charged atmosphere, and although I was waving and smiling at the crowd, my underlying emotions got the better of me and as was captured on T.V., a couple of stray tears rolled down my cheeks. My pride for my country and myself was overwhelming and something I will treasure forever.

We then marched to our designated place on the field joining the other 3,800 athletes to witness the lighting of the flame by the top track Australian athlete, Louise Sauvage. So, after the torch was lit, the speeches were said and the games were officially opened, that's when the real show started. We witnessed spectacular performances featuring artists such as Taxi Ride, Yothu Yindi, and the timeless Kylie Minogue. She was the last performer, and wow, did she rock it. The whole thing was just amazing and words can't do it justice. Then finally, a spectacular pyrotechnic display lit up the sky and the enormity of the next two weeks started to sink in as I realised this experience would define my life.

Village Life

The village itself was unique. It was built specifically to house the Olympians and Paralympians but with the intention to make it into a subdivision post-2000. The accommodation was brand new and comprised of houses rather than the dormitory styles of the past. Each country was kept together as a neighbourhood. Country flags were erected and so you knew where you were at all times – the bonus was that you didn't need a passport to travel from one to the other.

Our chef de mission had commissioned two stunning Māori pouwhenua (wooden posts), carved and blessed then shipped over to Sydney to become a gateway to the New Zealand village. It really was quite a spiritual experience every time I went underneath the posts, which also had the N.Z. flag suspended above.

The house I was allocated to I shared with seven other athletes. Other than my bedroom and the bathroom, I didn't spend a lot of time at the house so the kitchen and lounge area went unvisited. My bedroom was made up of two single beds either side of the room and a set of drawers for each person. The head and footboards of the bed were bright blue plastic. It might sound loud and gaudy, but it actually worked with the surrounding atmosphere. The quilt that was covering the bed was designed with the Olympic, Paralympics, and Sydney 2000 logos, and each member of every team who stayed in the village got to keep it.

The athlete I was sharing the room with competed on the first day. Sadly, she missed out which meant she was then no longer competing. From then until the closing ceremony I never saw her again. This worked out quite well for me as it meant that I had the room all to myself.

Next to the N.Z. office where the managers had their daily meetings was the medic area. This became a very familiar place for me not for anything tragic, but for the massage treatments I would have from the team masseur. Training for boccia had put a strain on my lower back and so at the end of each competition day, I would have a half-hour session which put me back together again for the next day. You might think this sounds lovely and relaxing, Reader, but it was more about maintenance and the management of a pre-existing injury than the cornucopia of diffused aromatic fragrances and whale songs.

Different sports start at different times in the Paralympics calendar. I think boccia had the perfect timing, as we were right in the middle of the two weeks. This gave us enough of a lead-in time to train and familiarise ourselves with our new environment. At the other end, it allowed us to have a bit of downtime and a look around at the other sports.

Our coach and manager were mindful of not training us too hard but just keeping the high level we had come to Sydney with. It was a very delicate recipe to achieve, but they maintained our peak form brilliantly.

In our downtime, we got to explore the village and all its wonders. On one side of the village was this huge, like really massive food hall that I'd ever seen. I'm talking three or four rugby fields of twenty-four hour food. It was actually not even a permanent structure although it looked like it. Anything your heart desired was on offer, and the food ranged from Indian to McDonalds and everything in-between.

Everyone had been issued with a coin. What a magic coin! You could put this coin into any vending machine around the village or stadiums and choose whatever you wanted. Once you'd retrieved your item the coin just spat right back out again as change to be used at a future machine. I could never look at another vending machine without contempt after that.

That food hall was located at one end of the village. Over on the other side was another complex called the International Zone. This had its own food hall with much more exotic foods and fewer crowds. Again, you could get anything you wanted, only this time if they didn't have it, they would make it for you. I felt like the queen. As well as the food on offer, there was a massive gaming arcade, movie theatre, and Internet cafe (all free) for the athletes' entertainment and use.

So the N.Z. Boccia team decided to make this a regular haunt.

On one occasion, we were at the Mexican kiosk, and Dad had piled food up onto one plate for himself and an athlete who needed assistance. He then proceeded to give one spoonful to my teammate and take a spoonful for himself (naturally a different spoon, duh!). As the meal progressed, my teammate became more and more quiet, red in the face, and starting to splutter as the food was piled in. Dad asked him a couple of times if he was okay – being a blokey bloke he shrugged it off and kept on eating. As the pile diminished, his agitation grew to the point where he was obviously in distress, and we thought we were going to have to give him the Heimlich manoeuvre. It was then that we discovered that the pile Dad was giving him was actually not capsicums but red-hot chillies. Why didn't Dad suffer as well? He doesn't like capsicums so wasn't eating the red vegetable.

I then said to Dad, "You can't kill him, he's a BC1 and needs to be on court at all times."

So, after training, we would go down to the International Zone to watch a movie, check emails or relax out in the arcade. Relax perhaps isn't quite the right word. When you get a bunch of CPs trying out the different arcade games it is a recipe for hilarity and disasters. One of my favourites was the skiing simulator. However, it soon turned to chaos when I was so immersed in the screen that when I skied down the slope, I actually fell off the cliff literally. Fits of laughter and then many hands putting me right back onto the slope again to repeat.

The foosball was another challenge with no co-ordination but my teammates were the same, so it made for a pretty slow and uneventful scoring game.

"Bloody funny to watch though," said the crowd.

The 'motorbike' was my favourite as I could finally sit down and relax while hooning through the mountain passes at high speed.

All Fun and Games

Down to business.

The competition was fierce. Eight of the best teams in the world ... and Australia (they only got in because they were the host country) hadn't qualified, but that's okay it was fun to watch them getting their arses kicked.

Once the competition started, I had tunnel vision, and nothing else registered.

Before each game, every athlete was required to enter into the call box. The athlete had to be there twenty minutes before the match otherwise disqualification occurred. It was a time for me to eye up the opponent. I did this by wheeling up and down doing stretches and keeping out of the way of any mind games from the other player.

We were also able to have our coach in there as well, so last-minute tactics and discussions were quietly held so as not to give the game away.

Just before the game, the referee would come into the call box and do a coin toss. It was funny because I was one of the very few females so I always let the guy talk first and nine times out of ten he would say "ladies first" and I was then able to call it … I actually won around 90 percent of the coin tosses … better than the N.Z. cricket team.

The competition was broken into three parts:

Individuals: Each player competes in a round-robin set of matches.

Pairs: Pairs are BC3 only which means that they play with ramps. (No N.Z. ramp players had qualified so there were no pair matches for us.)

Teams: Comprised of BC1 and BC2 players. The team is made up of only three players on court at any one time. This was our focus.

The individual games were first, and we were treating them as a warm-up to the main event – the Teams.

In the Individuals, I drew a reasonable pool, although I did have the world numbers 4 and 7 to play. My mission was to beat one of them in order to get out of pool play and into the last sixteen.

An excerpt from an email I wrote home describes the situation perfectly.

It's 2 days after we have finished competition and I still feel pretty shattered. Well um, how do I explain it? I'll start from the beginning.

I made it through to the last 16 in the individual competition by winning my last 2 must-win matches. I beat the Pom 6-3 in my first game before which I threw up as I was sooo nervous. I then lost to the Spaniard in the last end and that was when Keith Quinn interviewed me. They tell me that when it showed at home Paul Holmes had done a voice over on it - hilarious. The next day I played the Irish woman and beat her 6-4 and then beat the Norwegian 8-0. That put me in the last 16 and I had to play that night. I was a bit gutted to find that I had to play my team-mate especially as he had no games that day until then and I was absolutely exhausted. Anyway enough feeble excuses, he beat me and that was me out of the individual comp.

Referring to me throwing up – I was twenty-two years old, the captain of the team and at my first Paralympics, the pressure was immense. Not from any external factors but from within. What this created was a good old upchuck before any match. Nowadays there would be a sports psychologist on hand, however back then, it was me telling myself to put some breath freshener on and get out there and get it done. As I wheeled onto court, a switch flicked making the nerves and apprehension disappear, and in that moment I completely changed. I was in my zone, the world stopped as I entered an environment that is hard to put into words. Nothing else existed other than the court, the balls, and my opposition.

Now for the main event – the Teams.

Again, I'm going to use excerpts from my emails home.

> *In the teams' comp, we got through to the top 8 by beating Norway 8-2 and Argentina 12-4 and losing a very narrow game to Portugal 6-7. We played Great Britain the next morning in the quarters and beat them 10-2.*

On paper, it looked like we had cleaned up Great Britain which we had. However, the Poms didn't think so as at the end of the game they refused to sign the score sheet. (Both captains must sign this to make the game official.)

The reason behind this was that they incurred a penalty on the third end that had resulted in us scoring two more points. If you looked at the end result, we still would have beaten them.

Let me refresh your memory. Do you recall the farting incident at the world champs in New York when we were playing the Korean team? As you read on, keep in mind the rule that a team must be quiet during the opposition's turn.

The referee holds a paddle with red on one side and blue on the other. Each colour represents each team.

In this case, we were blue and Great Britain (GB) was red.

On the fourth end (six ends in a team game), GB had just played a scoring shot. The two others on court congratulated the player for such a great ball. They were quite enthusiastic with their congratulatory celebrations so much so that they did not see the referee switch his paddle to show our colour blue.

With the change of the paddle, the opposition was still Yeeharring, so I raised my hand in protest. The referee had actually not heard them as he was in the centre of the court and out of earshot. He called over the head umpire, they discussed the situation and it was decided to give us two penalty shots.

The Poms were furious.

So, at the end of the game when they wouldn't sign the scoresheet, we knew what was about to happen. Sure enough, they lodged a protest.

What happened during the hearing, we weren't privy to. Only the manager and coach of the protesting team were given the opportunity to argue their case to the panel. I felt it totally unfair that we weren't involved because we would have reiterated that the final outcome was way more than the two shots that had been awarded.

Back to the email:

> *We had to sit in the call room for a good hour and a half not knowing if we were going to have to replay the match or not. Held the programme up for over an hour and when the protest was finally thrown out, we had to go straight on to court to play our semifinal against Korea. Not the best preparation for the most important game of our lives.*

> *Not surprisingly we lost 3 on the first end and 2 on the next. I thought it was pull up your panties time and go home but we fought back to be 7-4 down on the last end. Gee, we played well at the end. With my 2 balls left to play we were holding 2. They had no balls left to play and I got another one in with my first which meant it was all tied up and I had a ball to play.*

That last ball will live with me for the rest of my life. Every time I think about it, I get transported back to that moment. I can smell, touch, and hear everything. As captain, you try your best to hide your feelings and gee up your teammates when under pressure, you also feel a huge responsibility to get the team through. I made a conscious decision to leave my balls till last so the pressure would come on me for any winning or losing shot, because that's the job description of a captain.

I decided what shot I was going to need to play. I lined it up. I brought back my arm and threw … *'Get in there',* I was saying to myself. The shot needed to be firm. I couldn't see at first whether the shot had made that intended target or not. As it was the last ball of the end, the referee invited both captains up to watch and measure. As I wheeled up to the head (where the balls are), I couldn't tell whether we had got one scoring shot (which would have tied the scores) or two (which would have won the game). I glanced at the Korean captain, but he gave nothing away. The head referee was called as they took their time measuring the balls. The first shot was clear, but my second shot and one of the Korean's shots were virtually identical. After about seven minutes of the measuring tape going from one ball to the other ball and backwards and forwards, it was decided that their shot was two millimetres closer than mine.

This meant the scores were all tied up at the end of the six ends. A tie-breaker was then needed. This meant an extra end.

The amount of time it took to measure gave the Koreans the opportunity to re-group. This ability to rise above a near defeat and go on to win that pivotal end is why they became Paralympic Champions.

I'll end with one last excerpt because honestly, I don't have any more words.

> *We then played Portugal for the bronze immediately after and had nothing left in the tank. We lost quite poorly and are feeling pretty devastated to how so close we came but no cigar.*

Immediately after the game, I didn't know how to feel. I went into the bathroom because I thought I was going to cry in front of Keith Quinn who was waiting to interview players. But when I got in there ... there was nothing, I was absolutely numb. Numb is the only word to describe what happened to me – I thought I should cry or scream or do something, but there was nothing in me as I had left it all on the court. I came out of the bathroom and it was like I was watching myself from the outside. I saw myself cuddle my family, I saw myself eventually catching up with Keith Quinn, I saw myself congratulating the players that had won medals, but I didn't seem to be physically there. It was a surreal and bizarre experience, and one I have never felt either before or since.

Eventually, I snapped out of this weird trance-like state just in time to be invited to the pub down the road by Paul Holmes and the All Black, Kees Meeuws, who had been flown over by the Rugby Union to watch the Wheel Blacks. The team used this time to decompress and pull ourselves together again.

We also bumped into the GB boccia team which could have been rather awkward, but to their credit, a couple of their players came over and congratulated us on how well we had played. These particular players also said how embarrassed they had been when the protest had been raised. It did make us feel a little vindicated.

We all made the effort to enjoy ourselves that night with the broadcasting crew and other athletes who joined us but it wasn't easy and when the night ended I crawled into bed with a heavy heart.

Not All Crips are Created Equal

I'm just going to slot in here an observation that I never came to understand until many years later. Please don't take this opinion of mine as a negative – it certainly isn't meant to be that. It's just an observation of mine of different people being put into the same box with the expectation of everyone being equal.

Let's be clear, the Paralympics and the athletes were amazing. The games opened my eyes to many, many things, one of which is that we crips are not created equal.

There is a hierarchical system that naturally occurs in society whether you want to believe it or not.

Well, the elite disabled sports sector is no different.

It soon became apparent to me that, in this hierarchical system, CPs and especially boccia CPs were right down the bottom of the totem pole. We were above one other disability, but only just.

Disabled sport is a society. I have already talked about how in general society assumptions are made when I'm meeting people for the first time. They think: you move funny, you talk funny, you must be funny in the head.

However, in the disabled sports society, this notion is magnified. Disabled athletes want to appear as strong and physically able to perform well in their chosen sport as they possibly can. Because of that, they want to maintain as much normalcy as possible. By bringing someone with CP into the mix, the pretence is too hard to maintain. I understand that. There was nothing overtly or consciously done by any of the athletes that would in any way be deemed discriminatory. It was more just an underlying vibe.

At the time that I was feeling all this, I didn't talk to anyone about it. It's only years of reflection that has made me realise what I observed back then was reality. I recently had this confirmed when I spoke to another boccia teammate who also had felt the same. It was definitely an inclusive team ... just not equal.

After the Big Show

After our games were over, we still had around two or three days left. We used this time to unwind and soak up the incredible atmosphere. We took advantage of our free passes to go to other sports and saw history being made when my fellow Paralympian and great mate, Dave MacCalman, threw the world record and won the gold medal in the men's javelin throw. It was magic seeing his medal ceremony and hearing our national anthem being played in the Sydney Olympic stadium. Very emotional.

We went to watch the wheelchair basketball which was dynamic and heart-pounding, then it was off to the sitting volleyball between Bosnia Herzegovina and Sweden. This was interesting not only for the unique sport but most of the athletes on the Bosnia Herzegovina team had been in the fighting units during the 1992–95 civil war and had had limbs blown off from mines.

Aside from Dave MacCalman, the other highlight was seeing the Wheel Blacks play. This is wheelchair rugby, fast and furious and amazing to watch. They also had performed the haka before their game that sent tingles down my spine. Needless to say, they won!

Even if we weren't actually competing, we were encouraged to wear our uniform. I was blown away by the number of people who would come up to me and ask for my autograph. I would say "Really??? My autograph???" It was a wonderful feeling to be so revered. I didn't tell my adoring fans that we actually finished fourth. To think that my John Hancock is floating around the world is, even now, quite surreal.

Closing Ceremony – Party Time.

The closing ceremony was the complete opposite from the opening. All the athletes could just wander into the stadium onto the track at their leisure and park themselves wherever they wanted. It was pretty cool just being out on the track. Dad and I had a mock 100-metre sprint and had a photo taken with us 'diving' over the finish line. Just before the actual ceremony started, the boccia team re-grouped so we would be together.

It had been a team decision to choose the flag bearer which I think is one of the biggest compliments that can be given in the Paralympic environment. Ben Lucas, a track athlete, was given the honour. In the closing ceremony, he alone came into the stadium with the N.Z. flag to represent all of us.

All the flags were put into their designated spots so all the countries were together.

The entertainment started, and it was like a real festival with huge floating balloons, kites, acrobats, and artists.

After the games were officially closed, that's when the party really started. Confetti rained down, massive balls were bounced around, and all the athletes mingled and partied into the night. I got out of my chair and felt the music as I danced all over the place. It was a freeing experience, but it was quite funny when some of the other boccia players from other countries saw me and said, "Hey, you shouldn't be able to do that," and I just said, "So who are you going to tell? It's all over." And just danced off.

It was such a natural high, no alcohol was consumed, but everyone was intoxicated with the Paralympic spirit.

Home

Arriving in New Zealand, we had no idea how the public had really got behind us and how prolific the media coverage had been. So it was quite a shock to be greeted at the arrivals. The medal winners were taken through first, then the other athletes followed which was just another reminder of our gut-wrenching fourth place. However, we came in like heroes as the crowd clapped and cheered for everyone.

When I got home, the interest in the games hadn't diminished. I was asked to speak at different functions and was interviewed a few times by the local media. It meant that it kept the buzz alive for me, and so the 'coming down' was gradual which helped considerably.

Awards That Slipped Through My Fingers

Let's just backtrack for a minute. In 1999, after qualifying for the Paralympics and retaining my National title, I was nominated for the Disabled Athletes Award as part of the Regional Sporting Excellence Awards. This was a shoo-in.

My nomination stated that I had captained N.Z. to a credible sixth place in the world and thus qualified for the following year's Paralympics. First in the National Championships and other regional titles, I had had a very strong year, so it all looked good.

The other nominees for this award had done well, but only on a regional level, therefore I, amongst everyone else, thought this was my year.

I invited my parents, grandparents, and close family friends to witness my victory ... we made a full exuberant table. I bought a new dress, got my hair done, legs waxed, you know, the usual stuff when you want to look fabulous in your moment of glory.

The evening arrived. We met at the venue and took our places at the table. Lots of chatter, lots of 'good luck' from well-wishers and it was all very exciting. My category got called and all the finalists' names were read out.

Then, "The 1999 Disabled Sports Person of the Year Award goes to ………." " OMG IT'S NOT ME!!!!! Burn!!!!

The whole table was stunned. I smiled through gritted teeth and started clapping for the winner.
But it was gut-wrenching, and more so when nearly every one later came up to me saying that I was robbed. It really taught me how to be gracious in defeat.

Now I know what the Oscar losers must feel like!

This was a very controversial decision which had repercussions for how the awards were judged in the future. The criteria became a lot more robust, and judges were expected to judge on the athletic merit and not any personal journey.

But it doesn't end there … My losing streak continued the following year, but this time, for a very good reason.

After returning home from the Paralympics and all the attention that went with it, a nomination was put forward for the Regional Sporting Excellence Awards but this time in the

Sports Woman of the Year category. You have to understand this was a huge feat as my nomination bridged the gap between non-disabled and disabled elite athletes in these mainstream awards.

I felt very honoured to be a finalist in this award, rubbing shoulders with non-disabled elite athletics. I knew I wasn't going to win this time as fourth place doesn't really cut the mustard even at the Paralympics. I lost to a golfer, who was brilliant, and it was well deserved. I believe she's even gone pro and doing well.

One awesome note, my Paralympic teammate, Dave MacCalman, who had won gold in Sydney, won the Sports Man and then the Supreme Award that night. This was another big leap forward in the history of the Paralympics in N.Z.

In with the Stars.

At the time I was playing boccia, the Paralympic movement wasn't sexy enough to warrant interest from the mainstream media.

A broadcaster, Paul Holmes, believed in it enough that he actually bankrolled the whole coverage of the New Zealanders in the 2000 Sydney Paralympics. He was to be the main broadcaster and he invited another two high-profile sports commentators, Keith Quinn and Martin Tasker, to join him.

Between them all, they put on a really good show that brought the quality of the coverage up into the sports news rather than a 'human interest' story as it had been in the past.

As I was captain of the boccia team, Keith Quinn interviewed me, so you can imagine how proud I was when he said to the chef de mission that it was the best interview he'd ever done with a sportsperson (including the All Blacks). I'm taking that!

As I said in my letter to my supporters, Paul Holmes rocked up to the bar the night of our defeat and was very generous in helping us to commiserate
A great way to end the Sydney Paralympics.

And so, to the 'stars'.
Back in New Zealand at Christmas time, Paul Holmes was in the habit of hosting elaborate Christmas functions where he would invite all the superstars of the year (sports, political, acting etc.).

Imagine my surprise when I was invited along with only the gold medal Paralympic winners. Why did he want me when I only finished fourth? Mine is not to reason why … I was going. So, it was off to the beauty clinic to get the legs waxed, the eyelashes tinted, and a bikini wax. Yes, a girl should always be prepared because she never knows when she might get lucky.

Man, what a fancy-pants event it was. I rubbed shoulders with Jonah Lomu (All Blacks), the Evers-Swindel twins (rowing), as well as the PM and other hobnobs and stars of the day.

The entertainment was Cirque du Soleil no less! Yes, it was one helluva night and the cherry on top of the most spectacular ride on the boccia rollercoaster.

Where to Now?

After it was over … it was over … what was I to do now? What was my purpose? Luckily, I still had my university to carry on with, and that became my focus. But it did take time to adjust my mindset.

People often asked me why I wasn't playing anymore. Why didn't I go to the next Paralympics?

I do catch myself from time to time wondering what would have happened if my shot had been successful. Would my life have changed? We never know which door is going to open, and sometimes, as in this case, we also don't know which door is going to shut.

After writing this chapter and reliving the emotional ups and downs of my sporting career, something has sparked my desire … perhaps the door is squeaking open?

mmmm is there another Paralympics in me?

9.

THE WORKING GIRL.

After I left university with a B.A. degree in hand, the question was, what was I going to do with it.

At this stage, I was still in Hamilton and wondering whether I wanted to stay there or shift away to new surroundings with new adventures.

Because I didn't know what direction to go in, a brainstorming session with Dad set us on the path to a new business, Roche Consulting. During my university days, I had developed a skill and passion for facilitation and advocacy. This was for the inclusion of disabled people in different situations.

Where this led with Roche Consulting was to develop a training package that educated the participant in the inclusion of disabled people in their particular industry.

That was all very well and good, but suddenly the onus was on me to actually deliver a quality programme that encompassed all of the client's needs as I was now getting paid for my services.

The leap into self-employment and having my own business was extremely scary and so, what better way to attack this than to contract my own father to co-present. We'd done this numerous times in the past for his work and we had been a brilliant double act. Getting him involved not only quelled my fears but also enhanced the programme by offering two different perspectives – a disabled person's view and industry knowledge.

Dad and I have always been an amazing team, bouncing off each other and giving such depth to the other's theme. This can't be learned. It is intuitive and is because we have grown together through the years.

The first, and I might add only, contract I secured was with a PolyTech. It was to deliver a four-hour workshop with practical components on the integration of the government's New Zealand Disability Strategy and how it pertained to the staff.

Nervous though I was, I was surprised at how well it went. Dad and I were, again, a brilliant team, but this time I was the one leading and it felt quite grown up.

However, fabulous though we were, this experience taught me that in actual fact, I needed more structure and security around me for my first foray into the workforce.
So, I started putting my C.V. together and getting myself out there to look for a 'real' job.

The First Job! I Got One!

You know how in the movies the hero starts at the bottom delivering the mail then works their way up to being the CEO? Okay so it didn't happen quite to the CEO point, but the bottom did!

I started in the filing room.

But before I actually started my new job, I had to make a major shift to the big smoke – Auckland City. This, in itself, was a huge upheaval and to add a new job, wow I was totally out of my comfort zone. But, up to Auckland I went.

My first 'home' was staying with a family friend, which made it a bit easier as I had a friendly face to come home to each night.

But the job itself was a really steep learning curve. I sure didn't feel like I was IN KANSAS anymore!

In the very first week when I hadn't even discovered the ropes, the boss said to me, "I thought you would have been better than this when I hired you".

This crushing comment has stuck with me and maybe that's why I always worry about people's opinions.

How I didn't get fired in those first few months in the filing room is beyond me. When I look back I think that I should have been paying them, but the learning experience was instrumental in developing my work ethic.

I soon realised that I needed help to perform my job description efficiently, so I got in touch with an agency that supports disabled people into work. Through them I began my life with a work P.A. and, as a result, I was soon out of the filing room and into my own office with my own caseload. My efficiency and productivity increased and so did my confidence and I was on my way to a fully bona fide career.

My first huge barrier was pronouncing the company's name as my job was to ring families up and talk to them about the services that they were receiving.

The conversation went kind of like this:

"Hi, it's Stacey here from (hard to pronounce company name)."

"Huh?"

"Stacey from (hard to pronounce company name)."

"Yes, I got the Stacey – but from where?"

"(Hard to pronounce company name). It's the agency that your child's services come from."

"Oh, you mean (pronounces company name easily)."

"Yes."

By the time I got to discuss what I needed to talk to them about I was exhausted. It was very interesting the reception I would get after this exchange. Quite often I would have the person refuse to talk to me as they wanted someone that could 'talk properly'.

To a fresh-faced, eager, optimistic university graduate like me thinking I could change the world, this was quite soul-destroying when they insisted that they wanted to hear a 'normal' voice on the phone.

As the person on the other end of the phone was a caregiver of a disabled child, I expected that they would respect me and value my point of view, but it was the complete opposite. They thought that I wouldn't have the skills to provide them with the services their family needed. This really shocked me and it was my first experience of discrimination in the workforce. I think that it was a reflection of how they viewed the abilities of their own child and perhaps it was too confronting to deal with me.

Everyone wants to step up and progress, and I was no different. I now had a new boss. The old one from the mailroom had spontaneously combusted never to be seen again in my burgeoning career. I talked to the boss about the possibility of going out to do home assessments. She was very encouraging, supported my request and assigned me a few different assessors to go out with to observe and learn from.

All was good until she assigned me to Gertrude.
Gertrude and I weren't close. She was very 'old school' and always quite condescending towards me but so subtly that no one else picked up on it. Her office was next door to mine and on hearing that she was to take me with her she contacted the client's family. It was a phone conversation where the volume

of her voice was, in my opinion, deliberately louder than normal. Consequently, I overheard everything.

"I HAVE to bring this person with a disability along to the meeting, will that be alright? Don't worry, she won't be contributing anything."

I was furious, as the tone of her voice had indicated to the client that she was being forced to have me there and implied that I was a waste of space. I felt outraged and discriminated against and thought I had a really good case to finally make people see that subtle undermining was happening.

So I went straight to my manager whom I thought would be on my side and would discipline Gertrude. Well, she did speak to her, but, boy, did I learn a lesson. The upshot was totally not what I expected. I was the one who was admonished for eavesdropping!!! I was back on phones full-time once more.

The phone calls continued with many other interesting and disturbing conversations. However, there was one that will haunt me for the rest of my life as I got told that if I didn't provide them with more support, they were going to kill their disabled child. Nothing ever prepares you for a conversation like this. To think that a family was in such dire circumstances to even verbalise such an extreme act in order to get our attention was a shocking revelation.

I instantly got an Urgent Needs Assessor to go out and visit them and then followed their case very closely after that.

We were funded by a Government agency who every year reduced the allocated funding. This meant my role was to try to take away some of the services the families had got in order to come in on budget, I would listen to these stories on the phone and it was gut-wrenching to then have to take some of their services away, it made me feel so helpless.

Note: This company now no longer exists.

Time to look for a new job.

Well, in reality, the job found me. In a roundabout way, I was headhunted.

It all started at my sister's wedding where I was the chief bridesmaid and was honoured to be I was asked to give a speech. This went down extremely well with the audience laughing and crying where they were supposed to and me absolutely nailing the delivery if I do say so myself.

One of the guests happened to be the CEO of the Halberg Trust, an organisation where my dad had a managerial position. This was somewhere I had always desired to work, but had never voiced it due to my dad's role, as I never wanted either him or me to be accused of nepotism.

After the wedding, the CEO, having listened to my speech, approached Dad and said, "Stacey needs to apply for the vacancy we have." Dad was rather surprised and they worked together on how this could be done IF I was successful (this was a big IF as the recruitment process was intensive).

To begin with, I was hesitant about submitting an application as I never wanted to compromise Dad's career, however, after I heard that he wasn't going to have anything to do with the selection and he was not going to be my manager, I set about applying for the position.

The first interview was intense to say the least. I was confronted with four senior executives who questioned me extensively about my experience and knowledge. I didn't perform well and was lucky to make the cut.
The next stage was that all the shortlisted candidates had to write and deliver an action plan for a fictitious sports club about getting a fictitious disabled person as a member of the said fictitious club.

I walked into the interview and instantly greeted them as 'committee members' of the club and congratulated them for implementing an action plan such as this. I then proceeded to outline what their club could do in order to facilitate this new member.

This approach was novel and the interview panel was so impressed that a couple of days later I was informed that the job was mine.

And so began my career with Halberg Trust.

Sir Murray Halberg, My Hero

I have met only a few people in my life I can say that have true mana, and Sir Murray Halberg is certainly one of those people. If you are unfamiliar with the Māori language, 'mana' is attached to someone who has great presence and prestige, and someone who deserves huge respect.
For me, 'mana' is the only word to describe Sir Murray.

He has such a gentle but commanding spirit, and his beautiful blue eyes can hold your soul and know exactly what you're thinking. It's almost a spiritual experience. I have never known or will ever know anyone quite like him.

To work for him was the biggest honour I could ever imagine. If you don't know who Sir Murray is, I'll give you a brief synopsis of one of New Zealand's national treasures.
He was born in 1933 and was a middle-distance runner. He won the gold medal in the 5000 metres event at the 1960 Olympics, which catapulted him into a celebrity status he never sought. However, it gave him the opportunity to establish the Halberg Trust in 1963. This Trust was to enhance the lives of physically disabled children through sport.
If you're wondering why he chose sport for disabled children, he had attended a function in Canada that helped raise funds for disabled children. This inspired him, and returning to New

Zealand, he used his celebrity status to establish the Murray Halberg Trust.

I first met Sir Murray when I was a child. I received funding from the Halberg Trust to buy the recumbent bike, Roche The Rebel, after which I went to one of the fundraisers to speak on how great the bike was. To meet the man in person was such a thrill.

So to work for the man, 'the legend', was the biggest honour of my life. It also meant that I was able to meet him more regularly, consequently, we got to know each other very well and became good friends. He never said it out loud, but I know I was his favourite.

When he came to visit the office, I would ask him for some 'Murray Power'. Just by being in his presence, he energized me and reminded me why I did my job and why it was such an honour to do it.

Back to My Career

I was with the Halberg Trust and then the Halberg Disability Sport Foundation for a total of eleven years. During this time, my role changed and morphed as I became more adept and experienced.

My very first role was working alongside two regional sports trusts to ensure all of their work included disabled people.

My previous job had been within the disabled community. Now I was working in the non-disabled community, and this meant working with staff to influence them to include disabled people. This was extremely challenging at times, but the fact that I was disabled helped considerably to show them that it could be achieved.

I was mainly based at Counties *Manukau* Sport, and this created opportunities to become part of their team, which I thoroughly enjoyed.

My first experience with CMS was an off-site planning retreat. The theme of the retreat was to come as your favourite music star. I went off to the costume shop and picked out Cyndi Lauper as I figured that she and I had things in common such as ... the bizarre.

Remember, Reader, at this stage, I didn't really know my colleagues at all.

So, on the first day, here we all are dressed as our chosen muso, and we're allocated into teams for a trivia quiz on music.

Because my teammates didn't know me, they were a little apprehensive about this Dribby Wobbly in their midst. I soon dispelled any false assumption on my intelligence as I proceeded to nail all the questions and even got the 100 point bonus that no one else got thanks to my love of the Bob Marley's Redemption song.

This sealed my place within the CMS community, and I have so many good memories of fun times with the staff, from Friday night drinks, to robust discussions about remembering disabled people, to being involved in all of their staff activities.

One of these activities I will never forget, as for the first time in my life, I was a netball player. Now a lot of scratching of heads was done when I put my name down to play. Of course I was included, but how this would be achieved needed a bit of planning. This was a classic example of how my work role impacted behaviour. You see, by virtue of my own impairment, I was the living example of modifying and adapting sports.

Another wheel chair was procured, and the opposing team had to rotate their players into it throughout the game to mark me.
I thoroughly enjoyed myself and loved being part of this sports team.

As well as bonding with the Sports Trusts, I was also lucky enough to be able to bond with my fellow Halberg colleagues who were based all around the country.

This was done each year when we had our hui (Māori for conference).

One particular time stands out as being more laughter than work.

Within every hui, the organiser always made sure there was a major physical activity because, after all, that's what we lived and breathed.

This time it was the ropes' course. To start, we had to climb a pole to get to the first rope. Now, my upper body strength wasn't exactly a Schwarzenegger type so the CEO was on hand to assist. By pushing me up by my butt (nothing dodgy just the biggest surface he could push on!), I started getting up the pole. Halfway up I began to fatigue and I needed to rest. What was there to rest on? Why, his head, of course. So here I am, a junior colleague sitting on the head of the CEO. Sealed my future really.

The next day we headed off to a sheep farm. Our team building exercise was to round up a flock of sheep and pen them. We were going quite well, we all had our arms spread out calling out, "Oi, oi oi, move it, get in there."
Suddenly, one rogue sheep decided to make a break for freedom.
The only thing in his way was my six-foot male colleague. But this was no ordinary sheep. He'd been watching Jonah Lomu and proceeded to literally run up and over the top of my still standing colleague.

We were totally awe struck by the feat of this animal and proceeded to collapse about laughing hysterically. Needless to say, all the other sheep did a 'free Willie' and followed Jonah to freedom.

That's enough details of my career at Halberg because there are more snippets scattered throughout this book. I will say, it was a time in my life that was incredibly fulfilling and I'm extremely proud of. I have nothing but love and thanks to all those I met and worked with during this period of my life.

I want to take this opportunity to publicly thank Sir Murray for writing the beautiful forward which appears at the start of this book. I think it does show just how much we value each other.

The decision to leave Halberg was probably the hardest decision I've ever had to make. The body was not behaving as well as it had been, and I could see the writing on the wall. Not one to miss out on an opportunity, house prices were soaring in Auckland, and I could see the best road was to sell up and shift closer to my family.

It was important for me to still retain my own autonomy, so I purchased an apartment at a beach forty-five minutes drive from Mum and Dad's home. A perfect compromise.

As for continuing my career, it's on hold for a while. Who knows, maybe 'author' will be the occupation I next put on my passport application. Watch this space.

10.

I'M LEAVING ON A .....

Australia

During my international sporting career (geez, that sounds flash, eh?), I met many sportspeople. However, there was only one from another country that I formed a friendship with. He was unfortunately, on the Australian team, our closest neighbour and biggest rival, but I didn't allow that to cloud my judgement.

You've guessed it … it's George from the boccia story.

During one tournament, he started chatting to me and suggested that I should go over to Australia for a holiday.
Naturally, I said yes as it sounded like such a great opportunity.

Once home, we communicated via email and phone and soon it was organised for me to take that trip.

He talked a good game and said that we would spend the turn of the Millennium on his 90 foot yacht and then go to a resort on a secluded island off the coast of Australia.
This all sounded pretty good to me.
I was in like Flynn.

I learned a valuable lesson.

Perhaps it was because I had enjoyed his company on the boccia court and we'd been great adversaries that I didn't listen to my gut telling me that this trip could prove to be disastrous as I didn't really know him at all.

So after a couple of hours with him, I realised I'd made a dreadful mistake, and three weeks were looming up to be a long, long time.

George expected things to be handed to him because of his disability. He wasn't a victim as such but played the victim card a lot, which didn't sit comfortably with me.

At the time I was at university studying for my future career. He, on the other hand, was still living at home with Mummy and Daddy and didn't appear to have any ambitious drive at all.

The holiday started with his family celebrating the turn of the century. As promised, it was on the 90 foot yacht on Sydney Harbour, overlooking the beautiful bridge and giving us prime views of the festivities.

It was bitterly cold and my party dress was designed for warmer weather.

Finally, we could go below decks and there the family said they were going home and asked us what we wanted to do.

All I wanted was to get warm and into a proper bed. George, on the other hand, wanted to stay on the yacht with his friends.

I went home with his parents, he stayed on board and any close friendship sailed away into the sunset never to return. His decision epitomised his self-absorption and sealed his fate.

However, there was still two and a half weeks to go.

The family went off to Canada, skiing. George and I, plus assistant, headed off to a secluded resort on a tropical island off the coast of Australia. Sounded like fun, but as I became more aware of George's personality, I realised that even the free cocktails beside the pool and the fun activities like parasailing weren't going to be a good substitute for friendship.

The only bright side was that the assistant turned out to be a really cool chick, and we hung out a lot together while George slept all day. The reason for his sleeping habits was because every night he would go off to the only nightclub on the island. One night I thought I would make the effort and go with him.

I arrived to find three flights of stairs going down to the club and George expecting to be carried down by the bouncers. Now his chair was a power chair and, with him in it, weighed about 150kg. Okay so he couldn't physically get down the stairs, however, it wouldn't have been my choice to expect people to carry me EVERY night ... I would have chosen not to go after the first time.

Once in the club, his routine was to sit in the corner and watch and wait for people to come to him rather than my approach, which was to dance and interact with the other patrons.

I realised that this summed up our complete difference of attitude when it came to independence and social skills.

This experience really showed me what my values are and the sort of people I want to have around me.

America - Home of the Brave

My partner at the time, Ringo, and I planned an amazing holiday to the USA covering New York, Washington DC, San Diego into Mexico (day trip to Tijuana), Las Vegas and L.A.

This trip was very much a 'game of two halves' the good and the bad interwoven into six weeks of fun, isolation, contentment, resentment, and the highs and lows of emotional turmoil.

There Were Three in This Relationship

Ringo, Paul and me. Who the hell is Paul? I hear you ask.
Paul was Ringo's best friend and he was on this trip as assistant to both of us. Helluva nice guy, but when those two got together they brought out the silly boys in each other.

Sadly both these guys had recently lost their mothers. In a way they were leaning on each other as they went through the grieving process. The two guys were able to share their common sorrow, something that I couldn't be part of and leaving me feeling a little isolated.

I had tried to connect with Ringo on an emotional level, to help him work through the loss of his mother. It was rather a double tragedy as his father had died a year before.

However, looking back, I see that he didn't want that and hence the reason he gravitated towards Paul with all the silly banter and none of the pressure to resolve his grief. I guess it showed the difference between the male and female psyche.

New York, New York

In my eyes, the previous experience I'd had with New York wasn't that good … I got urine on my hands, I'd been yelled at, and got stuck underground for hours.

So, what a difference fourteen years makes!!!

Mind you, staying in a private apartment in Manhattan, like four blocks away from Times Square, helped the situation. We did almost everything you can do in New York:

- Times Square.
- Empire State Building.
- 9/11 Memorial.
- Central Park.

- Shows on Broadway.
- Metropolitan Museum.
- American Museum of Natural History.

No horse carriage rides … remember, I hate horses!!

We attempted to row a paddleboat in Central Park, much to the enjoyment of Paul who was on the sideline filming our concentric circles that were getting us nowhere. He was laughing that much that he couldn't keep the camera still and the resulting movie felt like it was filmed out at sea.

The food was magnificent. Lots of street food, bagels, hot dogs, deli sandwiches, and tortillas … and, yes, I did put on weight there, but I didn't care.

Would I go back? Absolutely!

Move Over Mr. President, Washington DC Here I Come

It was summertime, and Washington DC was hotter than New York had been.

Ringo was a mad keen NASA enthusiast. Consequently, we trucked along to the NASA museum nice and early to get there by 9 a.m.

Let me point out that space travel doesn't interest me at all, but you do things for love.

Dutifully, I had gone along, nodded, smiled and made appropriate comments. But by 4 p.m, I was getting rather to the end of my tether.

At 4:30 p.m., the dam burst.

As Ringo was spouting forth about the moon landing, I cracked under the strain and in my loudest voice I yelled,

"And they didn't even land on the moon. It was a hoax!!!"

His mouth dropped and I stormed out … I swung the chair round with a flourish and out I sailed.

Would I go back? Nah – too boring – too hot!

Flying High to San Diego

The heat rose a couple of degrees.

Would I go back? Lovely place and great to say I've been there, but not a lot to mention so … moving right along to …

Tijuana

Hola! … OMG … Margaritas and tequila for everyone!!!!!

We were only there for a day, but what a day it was. Coming in at one of the highlights of the whole trip.

We walked across the border and passed guards with machine guns. Very scary looking dudes. Even though the borderline is imaginary, the difference from one step to the next is massive.

The land on the USA side was clean, pretty, green, and tidy. The Mexico side was brown, decrepit, dirty, and dusty.

However, once we got into the city the people made it strangely colourful.

For the whole day we shopped, ate, and drank and yes, it was amazing. The obligatory Mariachi band serenaded us while we had lunch, and they were phenomenal.

We posed on a 'zebra', which actually was a horse with painted stripes on it, poor wee thing. So even though I hate horses, I felt so sorry for this one that I donned the sombrero and 'jumped' on for the photo op.

"Five dollars, por favor."

I can safely say that I was pretty happy from the margaritas by the time we crossed the border back into the USA. This was probably just as well, because as we were waiting in a huge queue to cross, an officer came and singled us out, called to us to "hurry, hurry" and with that, we were chaperoned past all the other aliens to the front of the queue. If I'd had all my faculties together the "hurry, hurry" would have given me such a fright the Startle Reflex might have jumped in, and I could have knocked his machine gun and been in all sorts of trouble. Would I go back? Hell, yeah! More time and more Mexico would be brilliant.

What Happens in Vegas . . .

We arrived in Las Vegas to the craziest heat I have ever experienced. You couldn't be outside for more than five minutes otherwise you'd faint. In fact, step outside and it was like a brick wall of heat had smacked you in the face.

On day two, Paul hurt his knee, which inflamed a previous injury. This really put a spoke in the wheel of our mobility as Paul was the one to push my wheelchair.

But never fear, there are always solutions!

Mobility scooters for all of us ... wow ... awesome idea ... great plan. It must have been hilarious for onlookers to see three mobility scooters, driven by youthful Kiwis, hooning down the Strip.

But leave it to me to mess up a good thing.

After an evening's entertainment we headed back to our hotel. As we were not exactly in the best of neighbourhoods, we really wanted to make a hasty exit and so we floored our machines.

Now, I've introduced you, dear Reader, to two of my quirks being the Startle Reflex and the Spaz Grab back in Chapter five. Well, the next bit is an outstanding example of how the Spaz Grab can really get me into trouble.

The mobility scooter I was driving happened to have the accelerator on the handlebar. It was a small lever controlled by your finger to regulate the speed:

… pull it in = go fast, release = stop …

sounds easy enough until you incorporate CP and the Spaz Grab into the scenario.

My hand went into a Spaz Grab right when I was adjusting the Accelerator, and suddenly I was going full throttle. Legs flying in

all directions, screaming with terror, and trying to pull my crazy hand out of its death-like grip. I tried to control the steering as in front of me I could see a major danger. A likely deadly scenario loomed up and my life flashed before my eyes.

Off the pavement I went and into a four-lane highway totally out of control. Horns tooting, people yelling, cars swerving chaos reigning, and me and the mobility scooter flying into the middle of it all.

One vehicle had swerved to miss me, but the next one misjudged my chaotic driving and I hit it as it went past. Luckily for me, I clipped it on such an angle that the bumper spun me around and headed me back towards the footpath.

As soon as I got there, Paul was off his scooter and tackled me to get my Spaz Grab hand off the control.

The lady I'd hit parked her car and stormed over yelling,

"What the hell are y'all a-doin'? My momma's gonna whip my ass 'cause this here is huurr car ayn' you've dented it!" (The lady was obviously from the South.)

However, by this time, shock had settled in and I'm a screaming, jibbering idiot who no one can make sense of. She gave up her quest to get any financial retribution out of me, got back into her car, and drove off leaving me to my banshee wailing.

As we were still in the dodgy area, Ringo and Paul were really pushing to get us all into safer territory. I, on the other hand, didn't want to touch a scooter's knob ever again.

Paul needed to drive his one, Ringo needed to drive his, and I was left to somehow navigate the controls of mine. Amidst crying and with an incredibly tentative tap-by-tap with my index finger, we managed to head off again. What would have been a ten-minute journey took us two and a half hours.

The whole way back, I replayed that instant when I left the safety of the curb and I could see the headline:
"Crazy CP Kiwi Killed by Spaz Grab in Downtown Vegas."
I was too young and too pretty to die. All I could think about was how grateful I was that it had been the backside of a car and not the front of a truck.
Would I go back? Hell, no! It was a very strange place full of false promises and … near death!

L.A. Home of Plastic Fantasy

The only lovely part of L.A. for me were the theme parks. Here I suddenly turned into a big kid and set about going on every ride that I could.

Being in the wheelchairs, we didn't exactly get preferential treatment but on some of the older rides we had to be taken to the back entrance as the main entries weren't accessible. Ordinarily I would hate this treatment, but skipping a crazy long queue, I swallowed my pride and accepted the V.I.P. treatment. I did see some non-disabled people hiring wheelchairs just to cut the line.

As we would get into the actual ride, the staff would then take the wheelchairs around to the end and wait until we got there. Great service and the staff were lovely.
My favourite ride in Disneyland was Indiana Jones. I so enjoyed the massive boulder racing towards my face and, yes, I did physically duck, even after the third time, I was still ducking – but laughing.

Yes, I got souvenirs as one does, but the best ones I got were for my four young nephews. They were Mickey Mouse ears with each boy's name embroidered on the front. I kinda wish now I'd got one for myself.

We stayed till midnight until it closed. Wow, there were fireworks and Sleeping Beauty's castle was fully lit up with hundreds of lights. I defy anyone not to believe in magic in that moment.

The next day we continued the thrill rides at the California Adventure Land which was right next door to Disneyland.

Hands down, the best ride I've ever been on in my life was the Radiator Springs Racers. This was based on the movie *Cars* and it really felt like I was in the movie itself. It was like the Matrix, I knew it was real, but it felt like a cartoon. The ride was in an open-topped car and you were racing against another car, flying around the roller coaster-type track at warp speed. The detail in the scenery was phenomenal, and that's what made it feel like you were in the movie and the cars had come to life.

The font cover caricature is based on this ride.

Next was Universal Studio.

The obligatory tour I enjoyed, especially the thrill of the Jaws shark exploding out of the water and giving me a heck of a fright. Luckily, I wasn't holding anything as the Startle Reflex kicked in although the other passengers were probably more frightened of me than of Jaws.

Then to round off the evening we went to the Simpson's movie show. This was in a simulator theatre which I didn't realise until it was too late. I'm not good with the more gentle rocking and rolling of a simulator, give me a hard core roller coaster any day. So by about halfway through I was nearly ready to push the emergency button as I was feeling rather queasy. The motion gods smiled on me, and I managed to keep my dinner down and get through to the end. It was the last ride of the day and I was done.

Would I go back? Totally, as everyone needs to be a kid every now and again.

Six weeks was a very long time to be in a country where New Zealand is non-existent to most people, and let's face it, my romantic relationship was challenged. There were parts of America that I did enjoy but I have no desire to return. It certainly was great to be back in New Zealand.

On a Train Bound for Nowhere

The above title was a Facebook status I'd put up as a post at the beginning of the day. How prophetic that title would turn out to be twelve hours later.
This trip had so much promise and delivered the opposite.

I had just recently got engaged to Ringo and for a Christmas gift, I organised a weekend getaway to our capital city, Wellington. There, I had booked us into a swanky hotel, and we were going to do the sights and have some fun before flying home two days later.

The highlight of this gift was the express train we were to take from Auckland to Wellington, a journey that takes about 11 hours.

This was a deliberate move on my part, because just as Ringo loved NASA, he also loved trains whereas I'm not that fussed. I was, however, a bit worried about having to go to the toilet while the train was moving but that was my only concern.

The trip started well with the train arriving at the station in Auckland at 5 a.m. We boarded and got ourselves sorted. Ringo was excited which rubbed off on me … all was grand.

Not quite two hours into our journey, the excitement and anticipation completely evaporated in one horrific moment as fate took over.

We rounded a corner and there on the track we could see a cement truck. The driver was desperately trying to get his vehicle unstuck and out of harm's way to no avail.
The thoughts going on in my head were,
'The truck will move, the truck will move, the train will stop, the train will stop, we won't hit it, it will be fine.'
All of this is still so distinct in my memory and all of it happened in slow motion just like the scientific phenomena says it does.

At the last minute, the truck driver managed to jump clear and landed away from the tracks. Because of the angle of where our carriage was, we were able to see the train hit the truck and throw it up like a Tonka toy. Later I learned that there was a horrific twist as the truck had come down onto the driver, and sadly, he was killed instantly.

At the moment of impact, the jolt we experienced was massive. Luckily, I had the table down in front of me as I was perusing wedding magazines (my chosen entertainment), along with drinking a morning juice.

The impact threw the glass up into the air, the magazines became projectiles and flew off as my body slammed against the table. I wasn't hurt. Can't remember what happened to Ringo.

Because of the tragedy that killed the driver, we now found ourselves in a 'crime scene' and we were all detained as witnesses. It's not like we were going anywhere anyway, but it made the whole experience much more dramatic.

Police, ambulance and then the media all arrived on the scene, each with their own agendas. We were 'detained' for seven hours at the scene.
The media got the story out online while we were still there and that's how we found out that the driver had been killed.

Finally, a replacement engine arrived that shunted us to the next big city, Hamilton. There we got attached to another fast engine, and we were off again.

One and a half hours further on and fate struck for a second time. The train came to a sudden halt and we were informed that both sides of the track were engulfed in a bushfire burning out of control.

What the hell????? We're not in Australia. Bushfire? We don't have bushfires in N.Z. ... Well, we did that day! Holy moly, these were some bizarre circumstances piling up on top of each other making it feel like we were never getting to Wellington.
Another five hours stuck on the immobile train not going anywhere.

Just as an aside, I do want to say that the staff, during both these bizarre events, were magnificent. They rose to the occasion helping us with food and comfort plus everything in between.

After five hours of waiting for the fire to diminish enough to continue, it was decided that this was not going to happen and we would need to be bussed to Wellington.

Not likely!!! By that time, Ringo and I were totally over it and just wanted to go home.

So, everyone who needed to go to Wellington were put on busses, and those of us left were trained back to Auckland. We arrived at the station, at 3 a.m. a full twenty three hours from when we'd left!

I told you that it was a Train Bound for Nowhere.

11.

I LOVE ROCK 'N' ROLL

I love music. Music is how you define your mood and certain periods of your life. We all have our favourites and we all have music that speaks to us and I'm no different.

Concerts I have attended. Let's see.

The very first one I had tickets for was Oasis. It was in the 90s, and I was super pumped as I loved their music. I had talked my brother into accompanying me and although it wasn't really his taste in music, he agreed, bless him!

A couple of weeks before the concert I was devastated to be told that the band had broken up – Oasis was no more – the concert was off. How could they do that to me??? Even to this day when I hear an Oasis song, it makes me mad.

So I got my money back and invested it into the next gig, Alanis Morissette.
Convincing my brother to accompany me to this concert was a little bit harder as at this stage of her career, her songs were pretty much man-hating tirades, but being the good sport he is, he trundled along.

We were ushered to the wheelchair section, which turned out to be the best position ever! The crowd was standing, no seating for them, but our section had been purpose-built as a stage-like area above the crowd. This gave us a great viewing advantage and even more so for my brother who was standing behind me.

The concert began and the atmosphere started to build so by the time Alanis came out, we were all pumped, even my brother who didn't like her music. The next thing I could smell something familiar. Even though I didn't smell it often or partake at that time, I recognised the distinctive aroma of pot. And sure enough, I saw a joint being passed around all the wheelies. That really livened up the action.

The only downside that this was my first experience of being in a massive crowd.

Now, Reader, this might not be that dreadful for you, but have you tried being seated surrounded by a sea of bums from those who are walking in front, beside and behind you? It really is quite claustrophobic.
I had to put my head up towards the sky just to breathe; it was like having a snorkel on with that small gap to get the air.

Other concerts I've been to:
Robbie Williams ... twice!
Imagine Dragons. Awesome!

Made to go to the horrendous Stone Temple Pilots and thank god I had to work late so I missed Metalica!

Both of the above were because of the boyfriend at the time – I'm not a bogun!

Justin Timberlake … really good.

Coldplay … loved them.

Little River Band … or as I like to call them, Little Rubber Band.

Cat Stevens … but more of him later.

And, guess what – No Neil Diamond! And he's been to N.Z. a few times.

But the BEST of all-time to that date was … drum roll, please.

The Rolling Stones

This was on my bucket list and a once in a lifetime opportunity. I had bought tickets for the then current boyfriend and myself. However, by the time the concert rolled around, the current boyfriend had become the past boyfriend so I gave his ticket to a friend who was pretty stoked.

The Stones were everything and more than I hoped for. This was Rock 'n Roll at its very best.

It wasn't just the music it was the whole theatrics and the sheer presence of them. When Mick Jagger came onto the stage, dancing and strutting like only he can, it was like he connected us all in a giant electric field.

My favourite moment was when he came back out on stage in this floor-length cloak made from red feathers and proceeded to sing "Ode to the Devil." Just phenomenal ... words can't describe this concert.

The only disappointment was that they didn't play my favourite song of all time, the one I'm going to be buried with and pretty much why I had wanted to go to the concert in the first place.

'Paint it Black.'

Gutted, but I still do get to hear it often because it's my ringtone!!!
I have to tell people to ring me just so I can rock out.

Another one on the bucket list was:

Cat Stevens.

Well, I thought The Stones were the best ever, but, sorry Mick, Cat now creams it (pun intended).

This wasn't a concert, this was a journey into Cat Stevens'/Yusuf Islam's psyche. It felt like he was telling me a story and I was the only one in the room. It was the weirdest feeling as there were over 12,000 people around me, yet he was singing and talking directly to me.

Putting the physical person to the voice I'd only ever heard on radio or CDs was pretty overwhelming. At the very first song he played, I burst into tears because there he was in real life.

This set the tone for the rest of the concert.

I have never experienced anything like this before. He not only sang all his great songs, but he wove the telling of his life story throughout his time on the stage with changes of scenery making it more poignant and magical.

He shared some really personal stories, and it seemed almost like he was unburdening his thirty years of silence. It touched and moved me so much more than just hearing songs by a beloved artist. He was giving me an insight, an almost spiritual journey.

Two stories he told will remain forever in my memory.

He explained his journey into Islam as being the result of a near drowning incident. He had been swimming and didn't realise that he had swum out just too far. There was no one around, he was exhausted, and he couldn't get back to shore. As he lay on his back he looked up at the sky and said, "To whoever is out there, I will dedicate my life to you if you save me." Just then a big wave came and swept him back into the shallows and he was able to scramble to safety.

Later that day, he was talking to his brother who had recently turned to Islam and was explaining it to him. That was his sign and so he embraced the religion and relinquished his music.

The other story that stuck with me happened thirty years later when his son bought him a guitar and told him that the world needed him. This was right after 9/11 and so he started playing again knowing that this was now his calling ... The Peace Train.

I hope this is not sounding too cheesy. What I gained that night through his words and music is hard to explain, but for me, it was definitely a soul-moving experience.

Needless to say – best concert ever.

12.

PAs I HAVE KNOWN

PAs - The Good, The Bad and The Ugly.

Caregiver, support person, assistant, helper, I hate all these words and refer to the people I employ as my PA or personal assistant and even write it in their contract. The reason why I find the above words offensive is that they conjure up notions of power levels. The words suggest these people are more powerful than I am and that they have more authority over my life than I do. For me, using the terminology PA puts it into a work-related balance of me being 'the boss' and the PA taking instructions and fulfilling tasks.

For example, when I invite people round for dinner and they enjoy a yummy meal, obviously I haven't done the actual cooking, but I take the praise as I have facilitated the process to occur. I use this statement "facilitate the process to occur" frequently in relation to the dynamics between the PA and myself. This reinforces the fact that it is always my decision and my input as to what gets done.

Apart from Fee, my personal scribbler, everyone else is a PA.

Keeping my life the way I want it to be and working with someone to keep my life the way I want it to be can be a real balancing act.

Reader, read that last sentence again if you want! It's an eye twister but should make perfect sense.

This is totally dependent on the PA's personality and how they respond to direction. More so as they get into the job and feel comfortable around me because familiarity can breed contempt.

Sharing ideas, I encourage to a point. However, sharing ideas can quickly lead to imposing ideas, and that is one thing I absolutely cannot understand or condone.

The virtue of this PA job attracts a certain person. They can be a bleeding-heart do-gooder, a controlling psychopath, or just a really good person, and I have had all three. But the difference between these three is like the difference between night and day.

There are two distinctive PA roles in my world, one for work and one for home. They are similar in the overall taking of directions; they just operate in different environments.

The role of the 'my career' PA is to assist me in my everyday work life. It's not a glory role and it isn't a role that the PA is acknowledged for (apart from me). The PA is there to make my life easier by doing stuff that I cannot or find difficult to do. If you want your name in lights, this is not a job for you.

I only want one body part of theirs and that is their hands I don't want their brain, that's superfluous to my requirements.

Over the course of my career, a few PAs stand out for completely different reasons.

The Control Freak

This was a woman who enjoyed power a little too much. I found it difficult to give her direction, as she would always say that she had a better idea. She would speak to my colleagues about my role, things she really knew nothing about but would make out she did.

During times that I would be out of the office when a colleague asked her a question, she was all too keen to give her own opinion instead of passing them on to me. She would take credit for things she had actually learnt from me and tell people that they were her own ideas.

Slowly, I could see the hard fought respect my colleagues had for me begin to deteriorate and knew that, if I didn't nip it in the bud quickly, I would lose my authority.

The way I dealt with this was twofold.

First, I took my colleagues to one side and explained to them what my PA's role was and how important it was for me to keep the balance of positions in their correct order.

Next, I then told my PA, in no uncertain terms, that it was not in her job description to be sharing her ideas with anyone. She was to stop using the pronoun 'I' as in reality it was not her 'I' … it was my 'I'.

Consequently, this relationship didn't last too much longer and I was soon on the hunt for another work PA.

The Drama Queen

As I'm a socially minded individual, I thought that I would give those who have had a rough road a chance to get onto the job ladder. I contacted my local Work and Income office to see if they had any potential, out of work, people on their books. The one they sent me was the most unique one I've ever had.

She (we'll just presume she is a she as she could have been a he) was definitely one out of the box.

Picture this. My new PA arrived looking like one would if walking the top end of K-Road (a notoriously, sleazy street in Auckland city). Her make-up was heavily applied and she wore patent leather boots with heels so high it added several inches to her already towering height. She also had on a mini skirt that was perhaps a little more revealing for our workplace as the dress code in my office was track pants and sneakers.

Think *Pretty Woman* … without the 'pretty'. Oh yeah, maybe without the 'woman' too!

The first workshop she accompanied me to was at a school doing sport. I had told her she was to come dressed accordingly. No! She rocked up in a glittery short dress, high-heeled boots to above the knee, full makeup, and hair and nails done to perfection.

As we walked into the gym where the teachers were, I could see the looks of 'what the holy heck' written all over their faces as my PA followed behind me. A real freak show – a crip and a queen. I wish YouTube had been around in those days – we would have gone viral!

Back at the office, I called her into a meeting room, and as diplomatically as I could, I tried to make it clear that her 'dress code' was not appropriate for this environment.

Wow! Talk about 'Drama Queen'! She stormed out much to the amusement of the rest of the office and yelled out, "I CAN'T HANDLE THIS!"
One of my colleagues politely opened the door for her and waved Bye-bye.

Royalty had left my theatre forever.

Another couple of standout candidates in my work life are memorable for different reasons.

Global Warming

This was a woman must have been in her 70s. Nice enough lady. Had to teach her about computers, but she took to it pretty well.

A couple of weeks went past with no incident; in fact, I was starting to really enjoy having her as my PA and was getting lulled into a false sense of security. I should not have relaxed so much as suddenly the mask came off.

We were having lunch together randomly talking about life in general when she came out with a statement that really floored me.

"You know that global warming is not real, don't you?"
"What?" What on earth was she talking about?

Now, I wouldn't call myself a tree-hugger, but I am very aware and try to do my bit for the environment. So this statement was really out of left field, and I couldn't let it go.

We then proceeded to have a robust discussion that turned into a full-on rant from this elderly woman in the middle of the lunchroom and in front of my co-workers. Because she wouldn't stop, I took her into a meeting room to carry on away from my bemused colleagues who were having hysterics over this rather heated topic.

I tried to be the bigger person and say let's agree to disagree so we could carry on with work. However, she just wouldn't let it go, and at every opportunity she would reiterate her beliefs.

In the end, my patience started melting, and like the ice shelf, she inevitably slipped into the proverbial ocean never to be seen again.

Can't Spell

Now, in the role as my work PA it is pretty vital that one has the ability to grasp the English language. There was a lot of dictation, computer work, and note taking at meetings to be later transcribed.

So, my next PA could be called a bit of a disaster.
She came to me bright-eyed and bushy-tailed and singing her own praises with all the fabulous stuff she could do. It really didn't occur to me to give her a spelling test! She was so bad at twisting words around and getting them wrong that even the spellcheck on the computer gave up in the end.
Now, I'm not exactly the best speller in the world, in fact I'm rather bad at it, therefore it is one of the biggest parts of the PA's role and I rely on them to get the spelling right.
On one particular occasion, I had dictated to her a well put together report that I was actually really proud of. I had taken a lot of time and thought over the contents and all my research was well founded.

So I was absolutely mortified when my boss brought the report to me and showed me all the hundreds of spelling mistakes and misplaced words. The worst and most embarrassing was the frequent use of the word erection instead of election.

Another one erased from the page!

Now a couple of examples of the Home PA.

The Fabulous Cook ... NOT

This particular PA was a rather large woman whose eating requirements differed quite dramatically from my own.

You see one of the roles involved in being my home PA is to cook the meals. I'm too wobbly to be near a stove, no one wants dribbly in their food and ... "stay away from knives", I can still hear my mother say.

This PA's meals, in the beginning, were okay. But then she started supplementing with takeaway food.

I've always tried to maintain a healthy diet with only an odd treat of fast food, so at the start when it was infrequent, I didn't mind too much. However, it soon became a daily occurrence bringing fish and chips, Chinese, McDonald's and other fast food gourmet delights. But the last straw was when she brought with her KFC declaring, "This is my favourite meal" while she proceeded to open the boxes expecting me to use my hands and dig in. This particular chicken I absolutely abhor! Aside from the food, I was sorry to see her go, but my clothes were starting to shrink and I knew something had to give.

The God-Botherer

At this time, I was getting my PAs through an agency. When they arrived, they were to use my phone to call the agency to confirm they had started work, then phone again just before they left. I found this to be so rude as the PA would barge past me at the door demanding I tell her where the phone was. No "Hello" or "My name is …." or any other nicety; it was straight to the phone to clock in.

This particular day another random woman came knocking at my door. Like many before her, she barged in and headed straight to the phone. Once she'd phoned in, I was then able to give her instructions. However, as she started work she proceeded to give me a sermon on why I should let God into my life. Now, Reader, do you recall the earlier story of 'God Will Heal You'? If you do, you can imagine my reaction to having someone preaching at me in my own home. Needless to say, I 'politely' told her to leave and suggested that she keep her sermons for those who care.

Dual Personality

With a home PA, it can be a very personal and intimate relationship, one where the boundaries can get blurred between employee and friendship.

This particular PA is a classic example of the blurred lines and how the relationship can become toxic.

At the beginning, Matilda seemed to fit right in. She was an amazing cook and conducted her other duties with care. Soon a friendship formed as it would because we were working so closely together every day.
What I didn't see was the subtle ingratiating actions Matilda was doing. Perhaps she didn't see it either, but when I look back, the manipulation that evolved came as a real shock.

I pride myself on being a strong, independent person who is able to run my household the way I want it to be run.

Matilda very slowly started to share her opinions. At the start, I valued and enjoyed her input, especially when it came to advise on clothes.

Many times, she would tell me that what I was wearing perhaps wasn't quite right and so the two of us would go shopping for me to buy new outfits. Matilda was all too happy to take away the old clothes, which suited me as I'm not a hoarder and didn't want the 'not wearing again' excess cluttering up my home.

Soon this branched into the home decor and her opinions got more commanding. For example, she would frequently tell me that she hated my artificial flowers and that I could do better.

The manipulation was covered with her always ending stuff with "I want the place to look better for you", "I just want to help" or "I just want you to look the best", and because of this, I didn't see what was happening.

Getting back to the flowers. Finally, I'd had enough of her constant criticism and I did put my foot down telling her that I liked them and she should really just keep her opinions to herself.

However, the commanding attitude got worse, and it was only because she was a good cook that I tolerated her.

The final event that broke the spell was over a simple case of leaving a light on. I merely mentioned it to her just to remind her that I liked to have the lights switched off whenever she left.

She lost the plot at this. She started yelling at me about how ungrateful I was and how much she did for me even saying, "How dare you hassle me about one silly light bulb."

I was gob-smacked, but I was as careful as I could be to try and de-escalate the situation by asking her not to yell at me in my own house. However, that just made it worse and she continued to rant and rave which made me come out fighting from the corner she'd backed me into.

I eventually asked her to leave and that I was terminating the employment (we didn't have a contract – my bad). She then completely took leave of her senses and started screaming at me saying that until I paid her a month's salary in advance, she wasn't going to give me my house key or my eftpos (bank) card back. (As she did my grocery shopping she had access to my eftpos card and pin number.)

She then stormed out.

The first thing I did was phone my neighbours. They immediately came over, which helped me to relax so I could think straight about what I was going to do.

The thoughts whirling around in my head were that not only was she unhinged but she was in possession of my house key. She could come into my house at night and kill me while I slept. Or she could go and empty out my bank account. I needed to get them back. Mind you, I quickly went online and transferred all the money out of that account just in case.

Stuff goes bad, who you gunna call? ... Dad Busters!! He'll know what to do and he didn't let me down.

I think it's okay to not always solve your problems on your own. It is okay to ask for help as sometimes a cooler head provides better answers.

He firstly rang Matilda, but when she tried to tell her story about how terrible I was, Dad wasn't having any of it saying, "I don't give a damn what went down, you have stolen property and you need to give it back. You have one hour until I go to the police."

She then started to text me saying how horrible I was putting my dad onto her, that she hadn't done anything to deserve this and that she was the victim here. OMG, what a psychopath! Within an hour, I had about a dozen texts from her, all of them worse than the one before. It took all my self-control not to respond as I knew that doing so would only fuel the fire. I was trying to be the bigger person and not drop to her level, but it was damn hard!!!

The standoff continued. Dad went to the police after the hour was up, however, their hands were tied for twenty-four hours, not that we were about to tell Matilda.

Perhaps the cool, calming winds of logic reached her as the next day she arrived on the neighbours' doorstep with the key and card. She was about to plead her case when my neighbour grabbed the stuff off her and slammed the door in her face. It was nice to know my neighbours had my back.

Not only was I angry at this nasty situation, I was also ashamed that I had not seen how manipulative this woman was and that I had let it go on for so long.
However, I now see how easily people can get sucked in by supposedly trusting, kind, empathetic individuals who enjoy the control. It's also interesting how these control freaks' demeanour changes when they are challenged.

I pride myself on living within a routine, being on time, being clean and tidy, and maintaining my independence through my PA, which is a paradox in itself. I can't be independent without being dependent. So when the lightning strikes and the PA spontaneously combusts and leaves my life I can see my carefully orchestrated world crumble. I know this sounds very melodramatic but it feels like the domino effect. One falls which causes others to fall as well. The longer I'm without a PA, the more dominos fall until there's nothing left around me but chaos. I've come to realise that I have slight O.C.D., which just seems to heighten the chaos around me.

These experiences have definitely changed me; have made me harder, made me tougher, made me a little bit more wary and untrusting.. I'm also very cynical and now find myself questioning peoples' intentions, and it has become second nature to wonder what the person's motive is. I'm always seeing and expecting the worst from people. I don't want to be like this, but the system and the people within it have shifted my view on the world.

I'm going to end this chapter on an up-note, Reader. When you find a good PA, your world clicks. Everything is easier, everything is lighter, and the environment you live in is happier. I am always striving to achieve this. Life with PAs is a bit of a revolving door, they come in with sunshine and ease, but now I know when it's time to for them to leave before the thunder comes and chaos 'rains'.

13.

THE BLACK DOG

Okay, Reader, I know that so far this book has been mostly light and funny. Now, if this is all you're wanting, I suggest that you skip this chapter, as I will be doing just that once it's been written.

Even the word 'depression' I struggle with and prefer to use the saying 'the Black Dog'. I don't know why, but it just seems less scary and less severe. I think by now, Reader, you'll know that I'm all about words.

Looking back, there have been two rather large Black Dogs that have impacted my life, and both are due to a common theme.

I've had two totally committed relationships; both times I was completely and utterly in love with the particular guy and both times they decided to leave. Let's not get bogged down with the why because that's irrelevant as it's my resulting emotions that I want to talk about in this chapter. Enter the Black Dog.

The first time, I was surprised at how vicious the Black Dog could bite. It was a major shock, as I'd never been that vulnerable before. However, I did have some help and with a few counselling sessions, friends to lean on and an unexpected anchor, my own self-worth soon returned.

My mother was talking to a friend of hers and telling her that I was struggling after a breakup. This friend said her daughter had gone through a similar situation and that a poem really helped her.

So this poem came to me in a roundabout sort of a way. It really resonated with me, and it was something I could hold onto. I would read it constantly, and more so at night when it was the darkest for me. I made myself read it out loud to try and get outside my head. Something about it seemed to soothe my soul but it didn't last long and that's why I had to constantly read it over and over and over again.

To this day, if I find myself in a bad headspace, this poem is never far away from my reach, and it still has the same soothing effect. It continues to be my anchor.

After A While – by Veronica A. Shoffstall

> *After a while you learn the subtle difference between*
> *Holding a hand and chaining a soul*
> *And you learn that love doesn't mean leaning*
> *And you learn that kisses aren't contracts*
> *And presents aren't promises*
> *And you begin to accept your defeats*

With your head up and your eyes ahead

With the grace of a woman, not the grief of a child

And you learn to build all your roads on today because

Tomorrow's ground is too uncertain for plans

And futures have a way of falling down in mid-flight

So you plant your own garden, and decorate your own soul

Instead of waiting for someone to bring you flowers

And you learn that you really are strong

That you really can endure, and you really do have worth

And you learn, and you learn

With every goodbye, you learn.

This first breakup was more about him wanting a bigger and better life. He didn't think that I could fit into the 'white picket fence and the shiny new car' lifestyle. This, and building his career was what was important to him as it equalled the 'perfect life'. So, having a Dribbly Wobbly girlfriend just didn't fit into the mould.

I should have seen it coming, but the blinkers were on because I was in love.

The poem helped enormously through the saddest time and as I was coming out of it, I heard the song 'Give You Hell' by All American Rejects. I embraced this positive, defiant song; singing it loud and strong, and soon I got my power back.

I'll even admit to changing an odd word to suit with lyrics like:

"When you see my face, I hope it gives you hell…."

"And you're still probably working at a nine to five pace I wonder how bad that tastes…."

"Now where's your picket fence love and where's that shiny car and did it ever get you far…."

sung at top volume all helped to heal me.

The second relationship breakup, however, had other circumstances in play that culminated in a horrendous bite by the Black Dog, which spiralled me into an absolute pit of despair and self-hatred.

Even though I wasn't aware of it, the spiral downward had already started before the actual breakup. This was because my mobility had begun to deteriorate and I had been falling more often than I used to.

These falls were becoming more a lot more frequent and severe. After one particular fall which resulted in stitches, I completely lost my confidence and my fear of falling was heightened. I knew I needed something to stop the falls and so Johnny entered my life. Johnny Walker is aptly named for my bright pink walker, the upgrade to the rickety one I'd had as a kid.

Why is Johnny Walker bright pink? Because he's a cross-dresser of course.

On top of that, my boss strongly suggested that I should use my wheelchair full-time at work as a black eye was not a good look in the office.

Not only that but the beautiful relationship I thought I had was ending and consequently resulted in a very messy breakup.

Love starts in different ways and for me, it was the cliché girl meets her boy fantasy way. However, it blossomed into what I thought was true love. On reflection, I should have left it at just having fun together, but I got swept up in my own creation of who this man in my eyes would be. His attention to me made me feel incredibly desirable, wanted and needed, and this was my downfall. I morphed him into my ideal man. I shut down the part of me that knew deep down this was a wrong match. I didn't want to see any of the red flags because I had created my perfect partner and didn't want to lose him. You see, love isn't necessarily easy to obtain for anybody. And love definitely isn't easy to obtain for this Dribbly Wobbly, so when it came to me, I held on to it even though it wasn't perfect.

It's like that old saying, 'if you hold a butterfly too tight, it dies' but for me, it was like holding a bumblebee too tight and wondering why my hand hurt.

About four months into the relationship I became aware of something he was doing that didn't sit right with me, however, I swept it under the rug because I wanted this life so much. Then, two years later and with an engagement ring on my finger, the same action forced my hand, and I insisted that we get counselling sessions. I knew we were in trouble, but being the eternal optimist, I was committed to fixing and keeping the relationship alive.

The first session with the counsellor changed everything forever. Right at the start of this meeting we were asked if we wanted the relationship to continue. I said yes, he said no.

So being told in a cold, brown, dark office on a leather couch that my fiancé no longer wanted to be with me was as earth shattering as it can get.

We had arrived at the session in the same car, so obviously, we had to leave that way. As we left the office and headed outside, it started to rain heavily and both of us were drenched by the time we reached the car. Rather poetic, not that I saw the relevance at the time.

Now, I had actually kicked him out of the house a couple of days beforehand. In my mind, this had given me the moral high ground totally convincing me that the counselling was going to fix it all and we would be back on track heading down the aisle.

The devastating effect of his statement in that office caused me to try and hold tighter and fix it. So in the car, I gave him my power by saying things like:

"We can fix this." "You don't need to leave." and "I want you to stay".

He didn't respond to that, so I topped it off by asking, "Is it the fact that my mobility has decreased?"

What a stupid question to ask a narcissistic person who is looking for any excuse rather than acknowledge his own failings. But ask it I did, and his answer was "yes".

In that moment I lost something that took me many years to get back.

I had completely thrown myself into this relationship, becoming extremely loved up with a feeling of being completed and safe. As a result, my job had taken a back seat. My priority was the life I was building with him.

This produced some really hard conversations with my boss who was telling me that I had to pull my finger out and actually start performing or there was no point in my being there.

Getting back to that earth-shattering day. I had a hairdresser appointment to get a trim.

On the way to the salon I suffered major road rage, which I'll tell you about in a moment. I got to the hairdresser's, and sat in the chair, and told him that the relationship was over, in fact, I was no longer wearing the engagement ring. Nothing else for it … the hair was to be chopped off. Besides, I was only growing it for the wedding.

It was my way of trying to get rid of the hurt. FYI it didn't work!

Now for the road rage. I've always been an aggressive driver but consistently managed to keep it in check. However, on that day, I just totally lost the plot!

The car I was driving was a work car and powerfully branded with the organisation's logo. It was a vehicle I was always proud to be in because it showed just how much I valued being part of this team.

But on this day, the road rage took over. I tailgated, honked, and finished with a sweeping, powerful finger gesture that was very obvious.

Imagine my dismay the next day when I was called into the CEO's office to be reprimanded. I quickly thought on my feet regarding the finger gesture and blamed it on my Startle Reflex saying the driver had misinterpreted. It didn't really make much difference, I was still in big trouble.

The road-rage happened another few times and the complaints kept coming.

The powers that be at work were now really starting to take notice. They tried to support me but they were also acutely aware that they had a potentially dangerous driver on staff.

The first thing that I was asked to do was to take a driving test with an instructor to assess my competence.

The night before the test happened I cut my finger quite badly on a ceramic picture that had fallen off the wall. In my haste to pick it up I sliced the top of my finger which has resulted in a permanent scar.

The next day, finger bandaged, I got into the car with the instructor. The test was around half an hour and towards the end of it, because I had been gripping the steering wheel so tightly, blood had started to run down my hand and into my sleeve. The instructor noticed and suggested that I pull over. I wasn't having any of it, I had to get this done so told him that I was fine and we kept going.
After the test was completed he extended his hand, but when he saw all the blood on mine he quickly pulled away and just said, "You've passed, maybe go get that hand sorted out" and walked off.

With those results the boss decided that I would be allowed to keep the car but for the company's sake the branding had to be removed. Having to have had the test and then the branding gone it was another blow to my fractured self esteem. I felt I was a failure and wasn't worthy of representing this organisation.

The spiralling downward continued to get worse. I wasn't sleeping, I wasn't eating much, and after every meal I was throwing up to the point that I called myself an 'accidental bulimic'. Everything was hard, even breathing.
As time progressed, the nights became a terrifying place to be.

The sorrow consumed me, and I couldn't get my head above it. I cried all night without sleep. You can't function without sleep but that was what I was attempting to do. People said to me to take some time off work, but I didn't want to as that was the only place my thoughts weren't quite so loud.

Every time I opened my mouth I would start crying. People started avoiding me at work, as they knew the tears would come.

My whole world was falling down around me and I couldn't do anything about it. My beautiful job was in jeopardy, the man I had imagined I'd be growing old with had gone, and my body was not performing as well as it had.

What was the point …

I just didn't want to do this anymore.

I didn't want to be in my skin.

I didn't want my thoughts.

It was all too hard.

My thoughts were evil.

I was so mean to myself.

The darkness surrounding me meant I couldn't see anything else but that Black Dog.

It was everywhere and it was going to get me.

As I have already mentioned, music is one thing that can be a powerful ally for me, and so at this point, I latched onto a particular song by Christina Aguilera and Great Big World called 'Say Something'.

That song summed up the ending of my relationship and I played it over and over and over again when I got home from work and all night long.

Then two things happened that helped me to get away from the Black Dog.

My CEO had noticed my increasing despair at work and offered to pay for a few sessions with a Mindfulness Coach. I didn't immediately take him up on his offer but it stayed in the back of my mind.

At the same time, I saw an ad on T.V. by an ex-All Black, John Kirwan. He was promoting a website and programme to help people deal with depression, which is called, www.depression.org.nz. It prompted me to go online and take the questionnaire to figure out if this was indeed what was happening to me.

The result was affirmative.

I took up his advice and made an appointment with my Doctor the next day.

It was the weirdest thing. My Doctor pointed out to me that I was also suffering from anxiety as I couldn't look her in the eye, was constantly shuffling and my hands were moving around without conscious thought, not a tremor, just simply couldn't stop fidgeting.

My Doctor was fantastic and took the time to go through the options with me, but strongly suggested that I go on some antidepressants and sleeping tablets as well as seeking professional counselling.

Now, I've never been one to believe that I would ever need medical intervention for mental health. My mind is my strongest asset. Even when my body fails, I can still retain control over the situation with my problem-solving skills. But I was so far away from who I was, the Stacey that I and everyone else knew, that I took the advice and began the tablets.

OMG, the sleeping tablets, they were the best. At long last I could turn my brain off, not hear the nasty thoughts and could have a peaceful sleep. Oh, how I so needed to sleep!!!!

With the antidepressants, I didn't feel different, but I did, which sounds odd I know. It wasn't an instant fix, but I felt that something had shifted and I was moving forward.

Then came the counselling sessions. I was entitled to three sessions with a proper, hard-core brain shrinker. I was a bit worried that they would lock me in a padded room and not let me out. Flashback to the Wilson Home story!

But as it turned out, he was a really great psychiatrist who gave me some fantastic tools to ensure that the Black Dog wasn't going to jump on me and swallow me up.

They were good sessions however, this psychiatrist didn't see me at my worst and I knew I really needed more.

Throughout this whole episode, I had deliberately kept my friends and family at arm's length, not showing them the real depth of my despair. Perhaps I didn't want to let anyone down by admitting that I was unwell, vulnerable, and just that things could affect me way more than I thought they should.

The length of time that it normally takes to get over a breakup came and went. I was trying to get better, but it wasn't working, in fact, I was getting worse. And the fact that I hadn't allowed my friends and family in I realise now was very detrimental to
my healing process.

So, after these three sessions were done, I had enough sense to know that I needed to take up my CEO's offer of a mindfulness coach and continue on my healing journey.

It was this coach that helped me through the darkest times and literally saved my life. I was able to cope during the nights because of strategies he'd given me. You see, it was at these times that I wanted to get the knife out of the drawer or chuck the toaster into the bath. But his strategies worked … just.

What had always stopped me when I was so close to taking my life was that my family had worked so hard to get me where I was. How dare I mess their lives up by doing this? It was my love for my family and the absolute knowledge of their love for me that got me through those long nights.

I can't speak highly enough or tell you how much love I have for this mindfulness coach as he knew I didn't have too many funds and so after the CEO's offer finished, he reduced his rates because he knew I needed to continue with him. I thank the Universe for him otherwise I might not be here telling you this story today.

Even though I didn't allow my family to see the extent of my despair there was one aunty that read between the lines of my responses and knew that the pain was harder than I let on. She would text me every single day sending through an uplifting poignant quote. I hung onto these and at night would scroll through and read them repeatedly until sleep took over.

Slowly I learnt how to breathe again. I started to become aware of my surroundings. I had been hibernating for a year, functioning on autopilot, and just doing the bare minimum to survive. If you ask me what I did during that year I could not tell you I don't remember, and I actually can't recall events outside of the Black Dog.

A couple of big things helped me get back into the world. The first one came from my work. I had been struggling a lot with the position I held. My boss could see the potential in me and so she created a completely new role that targeted my skills. This was something that I absolutely loved, and I knew I was going to be good at it. This gave me purpose.

The second thing was exercise. I have always gone to a gym but during this time it became apparent that I needed it even more. I discovered that exercise cleared my thoughts and allowed me to focus on just the physical. Afterwards, the endorphins were just magical. As they kicked, in the real Stacey appeared, and for a brief moment in time I was quite euphoric.

Bit by bit the senses started to come back. That old cliché 'smell the roses' made so much sense. Music sounded sweeter, colours brighter, and the taste buds started to enjoy my food once more. It was like an awakening, and I could breathe again.

I kept my mindfulness coach because he happened to be an exceptional osteopath as well and it was quite handy as the falls continued. Every time I walked into his office he would ask, "What do you need today? Mind or body?" As time went on, it got more and more "body today, thanks" which we were both very happy about.

Many years later, the writing of this has been extremely hard but a very cathartic process. It has allowed me to reflect and understand the relationship imbalance and truly accept that the breakup was the best decision for me as well as him. I now realise that I am worth more than an imaginary picket fence.

From time to time a Black Dog comes to visit, but instead of shutting the door in its face and pretending it's not there, I actually look into its eyes and tell it to go away.

That Black Dog doesn't scare me anymore.

14.

POWER TRIPPERS FROM NAM

Being a disabled person, there are a lot of hoops you have to jump through in order to receive the necessary equipment to make your life easier, and believe you me it's exhausting both physically and mentally. These bits of equipment are over and above what anybody else would need to live their life. I'm talking about stuff like a wheelchair, bathroom modifications, rails, car modifications, you know, stuff that non-Dribbly Wobblies don't need to worry about.

In my many years of navigating the endless red tape that is the disability world, I have become quite proficient at knowing how to work the system. This is something that I'm proud of and ashamed of at the same time. Proud that I can get what I need, but ashamed that maybe I'm not the worst-case scenario of Dribbly Wobblies. However, this guilt evaporates when I see other crips walking around (well, I mean wheeling round) in Bling Bling wheelchairs and Bling Bling cars. I always said to Mum that I wish she'd dropped me on my head at birth because then the support systems would have been a lot more readily available. Anyway, I digress.

The point of this story is about the power trippers.

A power tripper is a person in authority that uses the said authority to make my life harder, more complicated and stressful! They know and I know that they are the gatekeepers of what I need at the time, therefore they wield that power like an axe above my head.

Funnily enough, all of the power trippers that I have met are non-disabled people. They have no idea what I experience on a daily basis, however, they try to tell me what is best for me, and that's the problem in a nutshell.

I will tell you the story of Tinky Winky later on, but for now, all you need to know is that it was my beautiful first car. After Tinky Winky died (spoiler alert), the hoops I had to jump through to get a new car is a prime example of the said 'power tripper'.

A friend told me that I could apply for funding to buy my next car that would suit my needs.

Into the office I went expecting to get guidance to navigate the system, fill out forms, have a bit of an interview and, hopefully, get approved.

Instead, I got a power tripper from Nam!!!!

The first thing that happened was her shock and dismay that I had got a car license without her department's knowledge and approval.

"What??? You HAVE a license???? How did you do that?"

My response was, "Just like everybody else, I sat the test with my local police officer."

"But you CAN'T do it like that. You're disabled. We need to give you the authorisation to be on the road. Who told you that you were allowed to drive?"

"My dad and the policeman." By now I was like a stunned mullet.

Apparently, these extreme authoritarians (I would love to use another word for them, but I'll keep my decorum), thought that they held the jurisdiction over disabled people driving, and the fact that I had by-passed them completely did not go down well at all.

"Well, this is just not good enough." she said, "You are going to have to re-sit your learners and restricted license under our supervision."

"But I don't understand. Why?"

"Because we decide who of you lot can drive and who can't. And, I'll be writing to the government licensing agency today telling them that your license is to be made null and void as of this moment."

Nooooooo!!!!!! I had done it all the right way. Just like my brother and sister I had learnt to drive with my dad and then sat the test with the local police officer like every other New Zealand citizen (I thought). But now this power tripper held the upper hand, and I had to toe the line in order to get my freedom back.

I just had to say, "So you're telling me that if I hadn't come to you for funding, you wouldn't even have known that I existed, let alone was on the road?"

She snapped back with, "Sooner or later you would have come to our attention and we would have pulled your license."

I was gob-smacked and I didn't have a come-back. I couldn't believe that she was implying the police officer did not have the capability of assessing my driving skills, when in fact, he'd been very complimentary of my prowess.

So, through the tests I went like the conformist they wanted.

But it didn't end there.

Throughout the driving test they added 'helpful' equipment.

Let me explain. When I first got my license, my car, Tinky Winky, was an automatic with no added modifications. I didn't need anything else to assist my driving and, honestly, still don't.

During the observation test, pieces of equipment were added to see if I found any use for them. What I didn't know was that as soon as I said "oh, that's quite handy" they would write it down and make it a compulsory addition on my license.

This means to this day, I am 'legally' not able to drive a car without these additional pieces of equipment as they are embedded in my license.

Apart from one useful tool, the rest were garbage and I didn't need these useless 'add-ons'. I still feel angry that I was manipulated and tricked into agreeing to all this extra equipment that I don't need or want. I truly believe they were punishing me. They were so incensed that I had bypassed their authority that they were going to teach me a lesson and make sure I could never drive someone else's car.

After a tedious, long, drawn-out process, I got my licence back and the needed funding for a car. I may have had to toe the line, but at least I got what I required.

Power Tripper From Nam – Agency From Hell

I think it is absolutely disgusting that, if you're not a squeaky wheel you're never going to get the oil. And even if you are a squeaky wheel, you get a bad reputation for being a troublemaker and consequently the hoops get harder to jump through.

In the early days of my career and living independently, I used to go through an agency to acquire PAs.

The relationship between the PA and myself needs to be on a personal but professional level. There needs to be respect, honesty, trust, and an overall good attitude to the job.
The agency that I had to use, according to the Ministry of Health, had their staff on a rote system, so I didn't always get the same woman each time. It was horrible to have to go

through the routine with a complete stranger nearly every day. As the PA was required early in the morning, this process made me exhausted even before I got to work.

The people who worked through the agency were paid the minimum wage and when I say minimum, I mean it because back in those days the poor things were only on eight dollars an hour. No wonder they had poor attitude and skils ... who would work for that money?

I've always been a strong-minded independent woman, this serves me well, however, the staff and their agencies don't want strong-minded people. They want people to tolerate unskilled work from disrespectful individuals who force you to listen to their beliefs and eat their sub-standard food. I was not going to tolerate this and complained to the agency on a number of occasions about the incompetent staff they were sending me.

I soon became known as a 'difficult client' and finally, the agency rang me to say that they would no longer provide me with any "caregivers" as I was too "fussy".

The power tripper from the agency who phoned told me that I needed to be more grateful for the staff that I was getting and show them respect. I then proceeded to say, "How about the respect I deserve in my own home?"

She came back with, "We are providing you with a service, you need us ... without us you'd be hopeless."

Those words were a red flag to a bull. Me? Hopeless? I think NOT.

So I responded with "Do not threaten me. I will be taking this further!" and proceeded to slam down the phone (we could in those days, they were manual phones).

I made a complaint to the Ministry of Health about that provider, and a couple of months later they got their contract cancelled. It appears I wasn't the only one who was a "difficult client".

And for once, the Ministry allowed me to be the power tripper and it felt dang good!

Losing the Agency all turned out for the best and I was one of the first people in New Zealand to go onto an Individualised Funding Contract.

This meant that I could employ my own staff and pay them an hourly rate worthy of their experience and commitment.

Dealing with all the different agencies is like walking a tightrope between what I need and what I'm allowed.

I still experience power trippers from Nam every so often, but now as I get older, they seem to be funnier, and I end up just laughing at them. Actually, it's the best way to diminish someone's power – you should try it some time.

15.

MARCH MADNESS

At the end of this book, you're going to read about how I climbed a mountain, but for now, I just want to tell you about the rest of that month which was totally mad.

March, of course, is my birthday month and this year was a momentous one as I was turning forty.

As I grew up, forty epitomised being settled, stable, and a real grown-up. You are meant to have a successful career, a spouse, a house and kids. It was one of those things that I always thought it would be like that for me. Maybe not the kids as I had already decided, years before, that children probably weren't on the cards. I'm realistic about my abilities, and looking after my nephews brought it home to me that even though I love children, it was not a feasible option for me. However, I thought everything else would be ticked off by the time I was forty.

Reality is a hell of a mirror to look into. Yes, I had had the successful career of which I'm very proud of, and I live in my own home, it's just the picket fence life that alludes me.

So, forty came around and I stepped into March deciding to do something really challenging and a bit crazy because I wanted to make up for the non-existent picket fence and to prove to myself that I wasn't just fading into irrelevancy.

By the start of March, I was well and truly into my gym workouts preparing myself for the mountain I was about to climb. The invitations for my birthday party had all gone out and as it got closer to the night, there was a bit of madness with the organising details. Then, to round the month off, I had been asked to be an MC for the awards ceremony as part of the Bay of Plenty Parafed Festival of Disability Sports.

So, let's start with the party.

I had told Mum and Dad that as I wasn't going to have a wedding, I really wanted this party to be a full-on celebration – ALL ABOUT ME – Princess Stacey!

They agreed to it and so we decided to hold it at their home, which is a renowned party location. Plenty of room to erect a marquee, lay a dance floor, get a real, live band, have plenty of food and drink, and invite lots of people. This party was to be bigger than Ben-Hur, my 'wedding' minus the groom but with all the rest of the trappings.

The dress. Of course, there has to be a dress, what's a girl's party without 'The Dress'? Mum and I went shopping. Honestly, a whole day was spent going around the shops trying on this one and that one and not liking any. I must admit

I got a bit deflated so we headed off for a very late lunch. Food helps everything. Across the road from the café, we noticed a Boutique that had recycled designer clothing. This was not something I had ever thought about, not because I'm a snob, but it just hadn't occurred to me.

Mum suggested we wander over and take a look. I was quite pleasantly surprised at the variety and quality of the clothing. So, armed with several dresses and outfits, I went into the changing room. An added bonus was that the changing area was big enough to fit both of us very comfortably, usually a major issue for a Dribbly Wobbly and whoever accompanies her.

I have fallen out of many a dressing room with my pants around my ankles and the person I'm with getting tangled in the curtain trying to save me. How dodgy a sight this is for anyone who has the misfortune of being within the immediate vicinity.

On the clothes went, off they went and were discarded. Finally, and honestly, it was the last one in the pile, I tried on the most gorgeous dress, and it was made for me. I wanted to use my wheelchair for some of the night therefore I needed the dress to be long enough so I wasn't worried about showing anything scary, but not too long to hinder the wheels. It also had to fit me comfortably so I could be free to boogie the night away. The Dress was black lace, little capped sleeves and it fit me ...

OMG, the fit was perfect. With all the work I'd been doing in the gym – wow, it paid off big time if I do say so myself.

The next thing to organise was the band. I suggest you get yourself a coffee (or your favourite beverage). This is going to need all your mental agility.

Dad plays golf with a guy who plays in a band. That band was unavailable but the guy said he would help. He then asked another guy if he was free, and that guy said yes but his band members weren't. Are you with me? So, this muso who plays guitar then asked another guy who plays drums in another band if he was free. Yes and he knew another guy who plays guitar and sings in yet another band. Hence a band was formed. A one-off, just for my party. No band name so couldn't tell anyone who they were, but they were all fantastic musicians, and on the night, excelled with a rockin' great time. It was my party and I'll dance if I want to.

And I did, for the whole night. I didn't even get to see everyone because I was on the dance floor, only taking breaks when the band did. But I guess everyone knew where I was, so if they wanted to see me, they had to come and dance with me.
Just like a wedding, there were speeches. Dad started it off as he is the family orator and everyone, including me, loved what he had to say. Then Mum stepped up to the microphone. This was a most unusual event as she is normally the strength behind the show. But she started speaking and within a few

moments I could feel the tears well up again. You see, she'd read me the speech the week before to see what I thought and that's when I really did cry.

The speech for me was so beautiful that I would like to share it with you.

> *It is very hard to believe that it is forty years since I gave birth to this delightful, gorgeous, funny, zany and amazingly talented young lady.*
>
> *When I went into the home to have her, we had no idea of the journey that we were about to embark on. I hadn't had a very good track record up until then – my first try of having one baby and then coming out of the home with twins – who knew what was ahead!*
>
> *Not long after having Stacey, I read an article written by Emily Kingsley that is an amazing description of our experience. I want to share it with you:*
>
> *It's like this:*
>
> *When you are going to have baby, it's like planning a fabulous vacation trip – to Italy. You buy a bunch of guidebooks and make wonderful plans. The Colosseum, Michelangelo's David, the Gondola's in Venice. You may even learn some handy phrases in Italian. It's all very exciting.*
>
> *After months of eager anticipation, the day finally arrives. You pack your bags and off you go. Several*

hours later the plane lands. The air hostess comes in and says, "Welcome to Holland".

"HOLLAND?" you say. "What do you mean, Holland? I signed up for Italy. All my life I've dreamed of going to Italy."

But there has been a change in flight plan. They've landed in Holland and there you must stay. The important thing is that they haven't taken you to a horrible place. It's just a different place.

So, you must go out and buy a new guidebook. And you must learn a whole new language. And you must meet a whole new group of people you would never have met.

It's just a different place. It's slower paced than Italy, less flashy than Italy. But after you've been there for a while and you catch your breath, you look around and you begin to notice that Holland is a beautiful place. Holland has windmills. Holland has tulips. Holland even has Rembrandts.

But everyone you know is busy coming and going from Italy. They are talking about what a wonderful time they had there. And for the rest of your life you will say "Yes, that is where I was supposed to go. That is what I had planned."

But you don't ever dwell on it because if you spend your life mourning the fact that you didn't get to Italy, you may never be free and able to enjoy the very special and the very lovely things about Holland.

> *Stacey – you are our Holland. You are amazing,*
> *and we are exceptionally proud of everything you*
> *have done in your life. We love Holland!*

My fortieth birthday party was a night that surpassed my hopes and expectations. It was filled with fun, laughter, and love with friends old and new, immediate and extended family and so many people making such a huge effort to get to this celebration. All the people who were there that night are some of my favourite people in the world, and yes, my Personal Scribbler was there too!

Stage one of March madness done and dusted.

Stage two – The Climb. You will read this later on so I'm not going to give anything away, but it's good and obviously, I didn't die, I just felt like I was going to!

Stage three of March Madness was probably the maddest and definitely the scariest. Let's just back the truck up a bit. When I worked for Halberg Disability Sport Foundation, I had a colleague who became one of my great friends. When I moved to the Bay of Plenty, this friend was very much the town crier and sang my praises to all who would listen.

"You have to have Stacey give you a talk."

"You have to have Stacey on your team."

"Stacey is the best thing, such knowledge … she'll be awesome."

OMG talk about building up people's expectations.

The first thing that happened when I moved to my new home was that I was asked to give a talk to the Parafed Bay of Plenty members at their AGM. (Parafed BOP is the local sporting organisation, which provides sporting opportunities for physically disabled people).

The talk was received with much applause and I'd no sooner stepped off the stage, figuratively speaking, than I was asked to be a board member. This is something that I continue to do to this day.

Not only did I become a board member I also started the Tauranga Boccia club and became the coach for the team which boasts six players. Now, I'm not a Kumbaya coach who tells you that you're wonderful if you throw the ball in the wrong direction, in fact, I'll call you out on that. Actually, I had to get rid of a player because he got so aggro when he would not listen to my instructions and continued to 'do it his way'. I coach the way I play – to win. I teach the technicalities and nuances of the game rather than just how to throw the ball. I'm lovingly known as 'Coach Roche'.

Back to the boardroom. So, we were sitting around the table one night discussing how to grow our Parafed profile, when the chairman said that we needed to step up and become the leader in our industry. His idea was to run a multi-sports event. I immediately got onboard with this idea as I remembered many, many years ago being part of a multi-sports events weekend that encompassed the boccia nationals. The first, and only time that boccia was part of something bigger within the national disability sporting sector. It was also the best national competition that I'd ever been part of.

The idea grew into the Bay of Plenty Parafed Festival of Disability Sports that is now held on an annual basis. The first of its kind was set down for the middle of March, the weekend after my party. The sports that were to be involved were wheelchair rugby, wheelchair basketball, blind bowls and, of course, boccia. Boccia's inclusion was non-negotiable for me and I told my players they were playing in this tournament, and it was a fait accompli whether they liked it or not.

On this board, we have some very successful and accomplished people who bring huge ideas. We are all professional, know when to be serious but also know when to laugh. In particular, there is me and one other chick who, perhaps poke a bit more fun, talk more nonsense, and keep it light.

So when it came up on the agenda to select an MC for the awards dinner, everyone immediately said, "Stacey and Panda, you two are funny, you'll pull it off."

Enjoying a bit of adoration from my peers I immediately accepted without thinking through the logistics of what an MC is required to do. Oh boy, I wish I had thought about the logistics.

You see, as an MC you have to keep everything on schedule and you have to read a script. Damn! No one told me there was going to be reading involved.

Now, I generally have to get pretty creative around the reading of intensive material, and especially pronunciation of certain words and names, so give me a script and tell me to read it out loud, I will lose my head. Let's face it, you can't fudge names or rephrase them as you can with other things. So once I got the script, I managed to use word association, and all over my copy were prompts above names or other words I knew I'd mess up. For example, Bessy – 'Think of your childhood doctor' was written above. These helped considerably to wrap my head around the names.

What didn't help were the script changes that were made during the course of the week. Then to top it off, just a couple of hours before the event, I got to the practice run-through and was handed a new script. That put me over the edge and the brave face that I was showing to all my fellow board members cracked. I had to let them in on my dirty secret.

My fellow MC told me that she would have my back at all times and that I wasn't to worry. I felt the weight lift off my shoulders and I knew I was going to be okay.

Panda and I share a quirky sense of humour, and we wanted this to reflect in our banter on the night. It was a bit edgy and a bit controversial, but because we are two crips, we pulled it off.

We then sat down and wrote our intro together. It went something like this.

> *Panda: Now for those of you who don't know us, my name is Panda. If I look a little familiar you might have seen me in last week's Woman's Weekly … just sayin' 'poster girl for disability'."*
>
> *Stace: Why are you the poster girl? … You've only been doing this for five years … You're just a baby crip … I've been doin it for forty.*
>
> *Panda: Obviously you haven't been doing a very good job then ... And have you not seen this face???*
>
> *Stace: Woman's Weekly … Ah there's no street cred there, my friend … I was in the Herald and on TV3 news for my walk up the Mount the other day so you've got competition sister … look up Stacey Roche on Google, folks …*
>
> *Panda: For those of you unfamiliar with the disability world, we are all often labelled under the same umbrella ... just cos we are sitting down most of the time. But ,that doesn't mean we're the same.*

> *Stace: No we're not ... I'm a girlie girl, and she's a tomboy ... She likes big balls and I like small ones ... sports balls that is, you dirty minded people.*
> *Panda and I are the face of all disability sports.*
> *Panda: The language we use is not meant to offend ... it is us reclaiming the language of disability and using it for ourselves about ourselves.*
> *Stace: So, if during the night you hear things such as, crip, munter, broken-ass wheelie, blinky, dribbly wobbly ... it's just our way of lessening the gap between non-disabled people and us ...*
> *But know that we are working hard to live fully ... to be 'in your face' unapologetic crips! ..."*

The banter that went on between us kept the audience laughing. It actually turned out to be amazing, and we certainly were an awesome double act, so much so that the Mayor of Tauranga came up to me and told me that I needed to run for city council! Does he really want my humour to invade the council chamber????

The mental agility I had to have that evening was the equivalent of walking up ten mountains. It was fun, but I think the mountains would have been easier.

I'm going to end this on telling you about the proudest moment of the night. The award for Service to Disability Sports went to my own dear father. The work he has done in the disability sports sector has shaped the way disabled New Zealanders enjoy sport today. He has been a pioneer in advocating and ensuring that the rights of disabled people are upheld when they choose their sport. For him to receive this inaugural award just made my heart burst with pride. I'm one of his biggest cheerleaders, but for other people to recognise him as well was quite emotional. He had no idea, he just thought he was coming to support me, but it was quite the opposite.

16.

NOW FOR SOME LITTLE SNIPPETS
& RANDOM STUFF.

Introducing Tinky Winky

In New Zealand the right of passage to drive begins at fifteen, well it did back in my day. My brother and sister got their licenses both on the dot of fifteen years of age. However, at the same age, I didn't think I could achieve such an ambitious task and it really didn't even occur to anyone that I should explore the possibility.

Consequently, it wasn't until I was at university, away from home and needing to get from one end of the city to the other for boccia training, that I decided that it was time I learnt to drive.

My dad, who was working away at the time, happened to mention to a colleague what I was planning to do and that he was starting to look for a car to suit my needs. His colleague said he had the perfect car that would be such a great fit for me, so much so that he didn't want any money to change hands.

Dad took possession of the car, which turned out to be the smallest, sweetest, cutest little button ever!!!! A Suzuki Alto. However, Dad had to drive it for about nine hours to get it home, bless his heart. I really don't know how he folded himself into it, but I soon became the proud owner of Tinky Winky.

During the teaching process, which, of course, Dad was the instructor, he would occasionally give a very loud, sudden yell to see what my Startle Reflex would do. It would be a complete deal-breaker if I shut my eyes and took my hands off the wheel.

What he discovered was that my adrenaline would kick in boosting me to hang on tighter and open my eyes wider. This was the complete opposite of what I used to do when I got a fright, but something changed when I got behind the wheel. Being in the driver's seat, I was now responsible for my actions and this seemed to increase my control over any involuntary movements. Dad was now certain that I would be safe on the road.

Once Dad had given me the driving lessons and as many frights as he possibly could, it was time to take the test.

We headed off to the local police station and booked in.
I passed with flying colours, both the learners, written paper and then the restricted vehicle driving test.

I was now licensed to drive Tinky Winky.

The Death of Tinky Winky

Last year at university ... exam time. Driving to my exam extremely underprepared, and knowing that I was likely going to fail this one, I got caught up in a bit of traffic.

Suddenly the car in front braked heavily. Very proud of my reflexes, I managed to brake and stop in time to allow a small space. No such luck with the car behind me – SLAM – I was squashed like a jam sandwich in the bottom of your bag between the two cars.

Everyone jumped out and came over to me. I wound down my window and started to say "I'm OKAY" but the minute they heard my voice and saw my movement, the assumption was made that I was badly injured.

"Call the ambulance!!"

"Call the police!!"

"Call the fire brigade ... this girl is hurt!!"

It was irrelevant what I said ... the emergency brigade was coming.

Finally, the police rocked up, and the nice officer came over to check on me. I shakily said, "I talk like this normally but I'm allowed to drive, here, look." and I handed him my driver's license.

He said, "Sweet as, besides it wasn't your fault."

I then got out of the car and went to the side of the road with my phone.

Hell – the exam!

I phoned my lecturer to say that I'd been involved in an accident and wouldn't be there to take the exam. How's that for a great excuse!

Her response was that she understood, and she would allow me to do a verbal test over the phone.

I phoned back later on and will not confirm nor deny whether I had my textbooks in front of me, but the fact that I got a B+ on an exam that I was sure I would fail may give you a clue.

Now, it wasn't a bad accident but I'm sad to say the sandwich effect meant that Tinky Winky lost his life that day. I will always miss you, Tinky Winky (sniff, sniff).

The Birthday Surprise – A Tree

As you know by now, my birthday is in March and starts a week of birthdays in our family. I love my birthday, it's all about me, the one day in the year as I said earlier, I can be a complete princess and no one can hassle me about it.

So when this particular birthday rolled around, it was no different.

I was living in Auckland in my first home that I had bought the year before. For twenty-six years, my family had always been there or phoned to wish me a happy birthday, so in preparation for the onslaught of well-wishers (before the time of posts on

Facebook!), I set the alarm to get up an hour earlier. This would give me plenty of time to enjoy all the adulation and still get to work on time (I didn't have a PA, so the extra hour was necessary).

I got out of bed ... no phone calls
I got out of the shower ... no phone calls
I got into my pretty birthday outfit ... no phone calls
I had my breakfast ... no phone calls
I got into my car ... no phone calls

By this time, I felt dejected, rejected, deflated, and downright devastated.
Driving to work it suddenly hit me that I was alone,
♪♪♪ *"nobody loves me, everybody hates me,*
I'm going down the garden to eat worms" ♪♪♪
I burst into hysterical sobbing and howling, and as I was driving, this was not a good combination.

Before I knew it, my company car had felt my sombre mood and wanted to help so had voluntarily committed to take over the driving. Suddenly I found myself up on the curb, driving through the grass over the patch of wildflowers and completely over a baby tree, ripping it from its roots and stopping us both in our tracks. Silly car, not looking where it was going!
I quickly looked around expecting an angry crowd of tree-huggers with pitchforks to lynch me for the brutal atrocity I had

just committed. But there was nobody ... how ironic the aloneness continued.

> ♫♫ *"All by myself…….. Don't want to be all by myself anymore……."* ♫♫

Kept playing in my head.

Then it hit me ….

"OMG this is a company car, and I can't be fired today, it's my birthday!"

I reversed back over the mangled tree, got out, and looked over the car. Seemed drivable, so I headed off to the company's mechanic trying not to cry again.

The car was damaged and so I had to advise my work. Damn, it was actually Dad that I was going to have to report this to. He happened to be on leave enjoying himself on a golfing trip, and the last thing he needed was to find out that one of the staff had driven into a poor little tree. When he asked me what happened, I was in such a state, my reaction was to lash out (you always lash out at the one who is nearest and dearest). I told him that it was actually his fault because he hadn't rung me for my birthday.

Five minutes after I got off that phone call, Mum rang to wish me happy birthday.
Too late, the damage was done!

In retrospect, obviously life happens, and my family are busy people, so the fact that they forgot this one ... ONE birthday is really not the important thing, the important thing is that they all adore me.

However, since then everybody in my family has never, ever forgotten to ring or text me for my birthday. They always say that they have to otherwise I'll drive into a tree!
I've even had a message the day before telling me that they won't forget to wish me happy birthday tomorrow just in case it tips me over the edge as I may become an environmental hazard. I guess I've got to wear this one for quite a few more years yet.

FYI ... 14th March I expect a message from you so I don't drive into a tree.

Toilet Seat

Post to Facebook ....

Bad thing happened: Lost my balance and started falling backwards.

Good thing happened: Toilet was behind me ... so fell onto the toilet seat, which softened the fall.

Bad thing happened: Bum connected with the seat with such a force that it broke the back of the toilet lid, my back connected with the cistern and a crack appeared.

Good thing happened: Because I landed on my bum on the seat, I didn't hurt myself.

Bad thing happened: The toilet cistern started leaking through the big crack. (Pun intended.)

Good thing happened: Quick plumber provided a completely new toilet system.

My Facebook friends then really embraced the toilet humour and their comments took it to another level ...

Hilary ████████ OMG Stacey Roche!!! Really glad you didn't hurt yourself, mix more T with the G :)))))))

Karen █████ That's one way to get a new toilet I guess hope you're OK

Karli ██ Stace you're a dufus!! What'd that toilet ever do to you!!?

Carol ███ You are a natural stunt woman.

Kirstine █████ Just for you ... I researched it and everything, although no randomised controlled studies on whether it prevents breaking of loos ....

Kirstine ▮▮▮ It's your rock hard glutes from doing squats!!!!

Sue ▮▮ And not even drunk! Oh you do make me laugh. X

David ▮▮ So what you are saying is your toilet got a big Crack? Hmmm

Alice ▮▮▮ 💩 Stace! Glad to hear you're ok and that the toilet took the brunt of it! And niiiice now you've got yourself a new rim! ...

Karen ▮▮▮ Oh Stace. Only you could accomplish this feat. Awesome story!

Lyndal ▮▮▮ . Glad you're ok. You can count on me to not make any potty jokes XX

Stuck

Playing hooky from work came back to bite me in the bum ... literally!

It happened while I was cruising around a beachy suburb in Auckland one day after a meeting. It was just too sunny to go back to the office, so I decided to bunk off for the rest of the afternoon.

I arrived at the beach ready to lax out in the sunshine when Mother Nature told me I needed to pee.

Public toilets are always dicey places for Dribbly Wobblies on their own as there are lots of hazards you need to negotiate before you can even start to relieve yourself.

Right at the entrance, there's usually a lip to catch you off-guard and then once you've stumbled into the facility you have the small stall to try and negotiate into. Next hazard is the toilet paper. Some idiot has designed a crip-proof contraption that you have to hook your finger up into to get out a single sheet of paper. That means you're there for about half an hour just to get enough paper to wipe ... and don't get me started on the flushing mechanisms. Next time you go into a public loo, have a look and see what I mean.

The scariest mechanism of them all, however, is the toilet lock, which brings me back to my story.
With all this in mind, undeterred, I ventured into the facility and got myself into the stall in the women's area. By this time, I was quite busting and slammed the door behind me, locked it and proceeded to relieve myself.
Finished my business, attacked the roll of paper, pulled up panties, conquered the flush unit, and turned to the door.

HORROR – I couldn't unlock it. My biggest fear was realised. I was going to die in the women's cubicle of a public lavatory, eaten by rodents that had crawled up the sewer system and out the toilet bowl.

The more agitated I became, the more frozen the lock and the more spazzy my hand got. I couldn't breathe. But. Being a good Girl Guide I am always prepared. I never go anywhere without my phone as this is my safety net, and this was a day I really needed that net.

The only person who was nearby that I knew would be available was my work colleague.

First thing he said was, "How is the meeting going? You're still in the meeting, aren't you?" I heard in his voice that he was rightfully assuming beautiful day, Friday afternoon, she's done a runner.

I had to confess. But he was a trooper and came to my rescue.

Let me add here that I had been stuck in this toilet for around two hours, and in that time had heard some sounds I do not ever want to hear again, but I will leave it to your imagination.

My rescuer arrived, and to the shock of another woman who had just walked in, had to actually climb over the top of the stall, as there was no space to crawl underneath. He was a big guy, and there wasn't much room in the stall by the time he landed. In fact, I'd scrambled onto the toilet seat to give him space.

One look at the door, and ten seconds later he said, "It's not even stuck … just turn it this way." And with that, a flick of his finger and we were FREE.

I swore him to secrecy and this cost me more than just one beer at the pub that we wandered off to. There was no point going back to work for us that day.

FIRE ... FIRE!!!!

I'd only been living in my new apartment about a month when there was an incident that forced me to meet my neighbours in a very undignified and unconventional way.

I'll paint you a picture.

It's morning. Later than I usually am, I'm in the shower washing my hair and enjoying the quiet solitude. My PA is in the other room attending to assigned tasks.

Suddenly the silence is shattered by the high-pitched scream of the fire alarm.

NOOOO!!!, I hadn't thought of this happening ... and, double NOOOO, I hadn't thought of this happening with no clothes on!!!

I'm just going to interject this narrative by telling you that a few people had raised concerns when I purchased my apartment. It is on the second floor, and in their words, "Very impractical to survive a fire. Not very forward-thinking of you."

My rebuttal to this was always, "It will serve me well for a tidal wave as I could just float out of my balcony door. All I'd need would be my floaties ... my floaties being my survival kit."

Where was I? Oh yes, naked, in the shower with a screaming fire alarm in one ear and a screaming PA in the other running around like a headless chook freaking out. I felt like slapping her. Instead, I said, "Please calm down, get my shoes and my dressing gown, and let's get out of here."
So we did.

I always use the lift, but obviously you can't when there's a fire, so stumbling down the stairs with my PA in tow and meeting the neighbours on the way, the unthinkable happened – flashing occurred. The front of my dressing gown took on a mind of its own and parted like the Red Sea.
This all happened in front of people I'd never met before. Here I was trying to make a good impression and not scare them into thinking they had a crazy lady living in their building, and what do I do? Go and FLASH them.

A drowned rat, dripping with water, hair all over my face, honestly, I looked like I'd just stepped out of Psycho, and to top it off, my PA was a blithering idiot beside me being absolutely useless. I did manage to cover up but not before half a dozen or so of my neighbours had seen the 'whole' of me.

A couple of months later the building had a Christmas party to which I was invited. Drinks flowed and tongues loosened, and it was there that the episode was relived with much hilarity and exaggeration of events in the re-telling.

I did post on Facebook, a short sentence with photo of me in my dressing gown dripping wet on the roadside. The comments were so entertaining that I've included some here:

Robyn ████████ You need to install a fireman's pole.

Lusi ████ A firefighter needed to carry you out Stace.

Carol ████ I've put all the pieces together and have come to a forensic conclusion. I think Stacey "pulled the alarm" just so she could run naked to safety knowing some hot firemen would have to come and help...yes/no? She's sneaky that way. LOL!!! ......

Robyn ██████████ You just knew there would be firemen coming to rescue you didn't you Stacey!

Denise ███ Possibly not a sight for all. 😉 . Glad you were all safe though 👻

Gloria █████ What a rude start to the day!! ....

Kylie ████████ Anything to impress the firemen 🚒 aye Stacey 🙂

Karli ███ Oh no!! Lucky you've been gyming and 2 flights of stairs are a piece of cake huh!

Arlene ██████ You sure you didn't set it off Stace? Bahaha those firemen in uniform and all?

Janine ██████ Why does that not surprise me!?? Another classic moment for you!! Don't ever change lol!

???? What's with most of my friends thinking it was all for the fireman???? Oh they know me so well!!! The sad thing was that it was just a drill and no men in uniforms turned up.

My Attempt to Re-enact the Scene from Ghost

One of my all-time favourite scenes from any movie is the romantic embrace at the potter's wheel. So, when I got the chance to throw some clay, my immediate vision was to re-enact that famous scene from the movie Ghost.

All that was missing was Patrick Swayze behind me, but I could imagine him there and the music playing as I sat down to create a masterpiece.

Now, I forgot that Demi Moore did not have Cerebral Palsy, which meant that her hands could flow with the clay as the water moved over it while she and Patrick created their magic. My attempt was completely different. The very first thing that happened was that the side of my left hand glanced the side of the wheel as it was spinning. Consequently, I managed to remove a good portion of my skin. Blood does not mix well with clay and I doubt Demi did that even in rehearsals.

Then there was the clay itself. It didn't want to behave and flew off and ended up on the floor.

Do you think I could get it to resemble anything other than a blob? And when I finally did get it moving, I was so excited and thought I was so clever that my hand forgot to stay open and the Spaz Grab occurred. This meant that some clay stayed in my clenched fist squirting out through the cracks in my fingers and the rest flew off and ended up on the floor again.

Have you ever tried to create the hole in the vase or pot with your fist rather than your fingers? May I suggest that you don't even try … it won't work.

The instructor, a woman this time as it was not my luck to have a Patrick Swayze, was very patient with me. She would calmly pick up the offending clay matter from the floor, put it back on the wheel and tell me to keep trying.

I soon found out that she was a placid woman who really didn't like swearing, quite the opposite to me who was swearing like a trooper when all these blobs kept flying around the room. Where was Patrick when I needed him?

The upshot was I came away with a sore hand, a frustrated attitude, and a blob of fired clay which I gave to my uncle for a birthday present. He was so polite. I'm sure that that blob ended up tucked away in his garden somewhere.

The Perfect Response

I was at a New Year's Eve party with my brother's family and their friends whose children didn't know me very well.

The party had proceeded in full force, drinks were flowing, and the atmosphere was one of celebration.

All the children were playing together and enjoying the fireworks and waving their sparklers. So I joined in with them because I'm such a fan of sparklers. Let's face it, you can't beat a good sparkler.

I noticed one of the children looking at me with curiosity. It was obvious he had never met anyone like me before. I then saw him turn to my nephew and heard him ask, "What's wrong with your aunty?"

Without even missing a beat, my nephew replied, "There's nothing wrong with her, she has CP … you know, Combat Power on Pokémon-Go."

What a beautiful answer from a very insightful young boy. I'm so lucky to have such accepting nephews who just roll with the punches and love me unconditionally.

A Random Act of Kindness

I drove into a petrol station to fill up. It was the day before Christmas and was so crazy busy that my anxiety levels rose. I knew it was going to be nigh on impossible to get forecourt assistance, something that is a necessary evil for me.

Just as I was about to reach for my phone to ring for assistance, a guy knocked on my window from the car beside mine and asked me if I needed help.

I don't know why, maybe he saw my anxious face or saw the wheelchair in the back, but either way I was very appreciative of this generous act.

He finished filling up my tank and started to move towards the shop. I stopped him and asked if he would send out the attendant to collect my credit card, as they knew me here.

Imagine my surprise when he said, "I've got this." and wandered off. I was so floored that my mouth literally dropped open.

I then drove to the little parking bay, got out of the car and waited for him to come back out. I gave him the biggest cuddle, he just shrugged and said "Merry Christmas" as he wandered off to his car.

I have never experienced this ever before in my life … not charity, just a beautiful guy!

Flasher!

"Why does this stuff keep happening to you, Stacey?"
This was the response from Mum when I had phoned to tell her about an incident that had occurred that day.
"I don't know." I said, "honestly, you can't make this stuff up!"

I had been at a council meeting and had parked my car in the public car park opposite the building. When I returned to my vehicle, I noticed a beat-up car parked in the mobility park beside me without a mobility permit showing.

This is one of my biggest bugbears and I take umbrage at people abusing these parks. In fact, I have got myself into a few arguments that have become quite heated over the years. "I'll only be five minutes." This is a statement I've heard so often and it always makes my blood boil.

Anyway, this particular day I was feeling quite bolshie, put it down to the meeting I had just endured, so when I saw the guy get out of the car and walk completely 'normally' I felt I had to intervene. I called out,

"Excuse me, mate, did you know that you've parked in a mobility park without a permit?"

Always start with a polite comment before you rip into them.

BUT … he then turned and faced me, and I saw his 'crazy eyes'. Those eyes told me he was definitely on something. Ooops, maybe I shouldn't have said anything.

My immediate thought was 'He's going to stab me with a screwdriver or something'.

He yelled, "What's it to you, you *%$*# @%#?" as he advanced swearing obscenities at me.

I was in the throes of putting my chair back into the boot of my car so I couldn't exactly jump into the car and lock the door. (Mind you, I can't exactly 'jump' into my car at the best of times!)

I looked around and saw that there was no one to save me. OMG, I could see this ending badly with me dead on the pavement.

When he started ranting, I tried to de-escalate the situation by not making eye contact and just getting my chair into my car. But when I did turn around ... HOLY MOLY!

He had his pants down, penis waving about and him pointing at it yelling, "This is my disability, you &#$@*(!"

I immediately thought to myself 'he's not wrong there!', it was so tiny and insignificant. I knew it wasn't going to harm me plus he seemed to be taking more interest in showing me his goods than actually attacking me.

I still felt threatened, but this did give me the time to get into my car and lock the door.

He then wandered off into the public toilets.

I took a photo of his car registration and got out of there as quickly as I could.

Later on that day, I was telling the story to a friend who told me that I should report it.

"Are you sure?" I questioned. "It wasn't like he did anything to me."

"You still should report it."

So I did. That evening I had a visit from two burly police officers. Man, they looked good in their uniforms.

They were very sympathetic and said that they appreciated me reporting this incident, as it is a 'gateway crime'.

As I gave the description of what happened I said,

"And if I was him, I wouldn't be showing anyone as it was pretty tiny." Both officers cracked up laughing at that. I then added, "I'm very happy to come in for a line-up, I'm quite sure I'd recognise that penis anywhere."

When I gave them the photo of the car, they put it into their system and it immediately popped up belonging to a person known to them. This wasn't the first time this had happened and the officers were going to follow it up. As they left, one of the officers said: "And I will give him a ticket for parking in the mobility park as well."

I felt vindicated.

As I went to sleep that night, I was glad the day had ended, but it still was an adventure to add to the ups and downs of this Dribbly Wobbly.

17.

WHAT'S IN A WORD

I am very passionate about the use of language, and more specifically, the language around disability, so I made words my career.

When I worked at Halberg Disability Sport Foundation, I became the go-to person when there was any question about what appropriate words to use in a given situation.

There are two fundamental philosophies around disability. Here you go, Reader, I bet you didn't think you were going to get educated in this book!!

The first is:

The Medical Model.

This is shaped by the disability being the problem of the person, in that their disability is permanent and they have to come up with solutions to deal with it.

Words that are associated with this model are:
- Confined to a wheelchair.
- Needs help.
- Needs a cure.

- Can't cook.
- Can't do up her own bra (this one was said to me!).

This is a very negative model and can impact significantly on the person's self-esteem and self-worth.

It's termed 're-active' because it's dealing with situations that are obvious and deemed unsolvable.

The second is:

The Social Model.

This model talks about society creating the problem for the person to overcome. You see disability only occurs when someone can't do something that has been created by society.

For example:
- Badly designed buildings.
- No mobility car-parks.
- Stairs instead of lifts.
- Segregated education.
- People who insult my intelligence!

This turns the table around and gives power to the disabled person who is then able to find solutions in a much more productive way.

This is termed 'pro-active'.

I fully believe in the Social Model as it is a positive way of reacting to any limitations that I may encounter.

Nature vs Nurture.

The psychology of nature vs nurture is continually debated. The experts say the behaviour is either inherited (genetic) or acquired (learned).
Nature is what we're born with genetically and biologically.
Nurture is about what we're exposed to, what we experience, and what we learn.

Why, I hear you ask, do I sound quite academic for a change? Never fear, I am getting to my point.

I often think about nature vs nurture in relation to my situation and I often wonder who I would be without the external influences I experienced growing up.

I have already described my parents as being staunch in their belief that my experiences should be the same as my older brother and sister, but I didn't go into depth about how they achieved this.
So let's look at what happened.

Do I think they were hard on me? No. I saw them treat my brother and sister the same way. Perhaps they were a little more insistent with opportunities (even those yukky horses!!!), but that was for my benefit.

I classify the above as 'nurture'. So let's talk about the 'nature'. Pretty obvious actually ... isn't it?

I was born with Cerebral Palsy (if you haven't figured that out by now, what book are you reading???), but was I born with the fight already in me … or did that come with the nurture? That's the question I am exploring here.

For example:

It wasn't until I got to school and saw all my mates walking, that I was motivated to begin to walk. You see, I just wanted to be like them. Was this because, even though I'd seen people walking, it hadn't registered that that's what I should do? My knee walking worked just fine, then I observed kids my size and I realised I should be upright. This has to be under the 'learned' or nurture category.

Throughout my life, I have come across many other people who have also made me question the nature vs nurture.

For example:

One guy I knew had been dropped on his head as a baby and experienced something similar to a stroke affecting one side of his body.

Because his family were quite alternative (putting it politely), they didn't seek the mainstream medical interventions that were on offer, e.g., physiotherapy.

Consequently, his left leg cannot weight bear as the muscles have permanently wasted away.

Speaking to my sister who is a pediatric physio, I discovered that if he'd had specialised and intensive physiotherapy, he may have retained muscle strength and possibly been able to use the leg.

Now, my question is, if the decision had been made to go with physio, what would the outcome have been and how different would his life have been? I'm sure he'd still be the not very nice person that he is (just a walking one), which possibly comes from 'nature'.

Looking at my life, I'm convinced that I am who I am because of nurture. Certainly, nature has its part to play, but my experiences were a result of my parents doing their utmost for me so I would be the best I could be.

I've met a lot of Dribbly Wobblies in my life, some with awesome attitudes and drive, and others with sucky attitudes and no drive. Why is there such a contrast?
Their level of Dribbly Wobbliness is the same but their attitude completely changes their outlook.

Let's all sing Monty Python's Life of Brian song …

> ♫♫♫*'Always look on the bright side of life*
> *d'do, d'do. d'do d'do d'do d'do. (now we whistle)*
> *wh'oo ♫, wh'oo ♫, wh'oo ♫ wh'oo ♫ wh'oo ♫*
> *wh'oo ♫♫♫*

I get told all the time that I'm 'inspiring' and I'm 'incredible' and I'm blah blah blah, and all I think is blah blah blah because I don't see myself as anything different than my brother or sister, two amazing people who have accomplished huge things.

I think it's because I was nurtured to believe I was just as capable as them, and I still think that way.

So I wonder what I would be like now with different parents. Ones who wrapped me in cotton wool and let me give up every time I shed a tear and told them it was too hard?
I know what I'd be like. I'd be rocking in a corner somewhere being the victim and expecting everyone to fix me.
Instead, I am an accomplished woman with many strings to my bow, and I have seen and experienced probably more because of who I am and who I have become than many others in the general population.

Nature or nurture? ... Who cares ... pretty good life and I totally believe I am who I am because of my family, especially my parents.

Don't Call Me Special

Now I'm going to completely contradict myself ... it's about 'Say what I tell you to say not what I actually say'.

In my life, I have learnt that the use of language can either compound the heaviness of a situation or lighten it. My tone throughout this book has attempted to be light and I do this in a non-PC way.

I know that you're saying to yourself,

"Hey, that's not fair, why can she call herself a 'crip' and I can't?"

I put it to you that it is exactly the same as any other culture in the world and how they use different words to describe themselves within their own group.

As a European person, I would not use the 'N' word but Kanye West can.

And so this is why, unfair as it may seem, if you call me a 'Dribbly Wobbly' I'll punch you in the face!!!!

I have told a few people about the title for this book and a lot of them have baulked at the words and said that I can't say that.

… Oh yes, I can. Because what I'm doing is trying to lessen the severity of my disability and bring some light to a pretty heavy topic.

Also, to help you understand that there is a culture within the disability community.

A prime example of this is at the Paralympics. The PC police would have had a heart attack if they had heard what was being said within the teams' conversations.

We have the unspoken permission to call each other Blinkies, Wheelies, Wobblies and other such nicknames. But you can't, as it's not your culture.

Touching on the 'S' word. As we may find the 'N' word abhorrent I also find the 'S' word just as bad.

Even if my partner called me 'special' I would automatically get defensive and ask what he meant by that.

Because to me, the word special doesn't mean a lovely, unique person as it would to you. It means weird and abnormal.

So … don't call me Special.

Direct or Indirect Discrimination

Working in my chosen career where I was privileged enough to educate others about direct or indirect discrimination, it made me aware of just how much indirect discrimination is out there.

Direct discrimination doesn't happen all that often otherwise you get sued or publicly shamed. For example, putting up a sign 'No Dribbly Wobblies Here' is just too darn blatant a discrimination, but not acknowledging them as they come through the door is just as powerful. Sadly, people think they can get away with that, and they often do.

Perhaps I do see it more than others because it was such a big part of my career, however, it is there and it does happen.

Let me give you some examples.

If I am out with a friend and we go into a café, the person behind the counter will first ask my friend her order then will look at her and question what it is that I want. Instead of looking at me and asking me directly, the person assumes that I have no voice.

This happens in any situation to do with retail. I have got to the point now where I make sure that I get to the counter first and I put my order in, then turn to my friend and say "what do you want?"

Another example is the simple act of getting out of my car. People's eyes will bulge and their jaw drop as they stare dumbfounded at the mere combination of a Dribbly Wobbly and a vehicle. When I feel a bit cheeky, I will exaggerate my movements just to freak them out. Makes my day!

On the days that I'm feeling good, I'm happy and I'm one with the world, I just don't really see this type of discrimination. However, days I'm not in the best mood, or just had a fall or some other catastrophe, I see every single second look, double take, glance, stare, and ignoring that is done, and it makes me want to cry.

Because of my career and the knowledge gained through that, I have found myself to be more assertive than I would probably want to be, and sometimes it gets construed as me being bossy or demanding.

Here's the problem in a nutshell; they see my movements, they hear my voice, and they assume I have nothing worthy to offer. My assertiveness is just saying – I DO HAVE A VOICE!

On a lighter note. I had a short phone conversation the other day with a telco. She happened to ring me just at the wrong time as I was with a friend.
So I interrupted her and said:
Me: "I'm in the middle of something at the moment."
Her: "Oh, I'm so sorry to hear that. I hope you feel better."
WHAAAAAT???? Did she think I was throwing up?
Another classic case of assumption made.

Unknown Impressions I've Made

School Reunion

In my late thirties, I attended my first ever school reunion. I wasn't overly convinced that I should go as my memories of school were not filled with fun times or heaps of friends ... in fact it was the opposite.

My brother and sister convinced me, and I agreed on the proviso that I would hang with them and not in the toilets like I had most of my school life.
There was a huge turnout as it was the fifty-year celebration so there were students from all generations.

Right at the start, my sister found her classmates and we all started talking. Next thing, there was a tap on my shoulder and

I turned to see one of my own classmates had come over to talk to me. Suddenly, the floodgates were open and my peers surrounded me.

From that moment on, I was hot property much to my absolute amazement. Conversation flowed as we found out what we had all been doing with our lives. I had a queue of people waiting to talk to me and to buy me drinks.

Suddenly, I felt like I was the parish priest absolving the congregation's sins as each person recalled our time in school, and many of them apologised for how they had treated me. Funnily enough, even though some of the stories they were telling I remembered, I had never held grudges because, gosh, we were only kids and that's how kids act.

The years fell away, the isolation I'd felt vanished, and I finally felt like I was part of this peer group. It was the most unusual but beautiful feeling I'd ever experienced in my life. People were actually interested in me and were impressed with what I'd done in my life, just like I was with some of their accomplishments.

Needless to say, I didn't spend a cent. It was an amazing night and cathartic for everyone.

Who Remembers You

One of the boys at my school, Ben, who I really didn't know at all (he was in the cool group), was living in Brisbane.

He happened to go into a bar and noticed a guy in a power chair on his own in the corner.

Ben thought he recognised the movements he'd seen with me and wondered if he had CP. He got his drink then wandered over and started a conversation and by way of introduction, he said that he was from New Zealand. The Aussie was taken aback by Ben's approach as he wasn't used to anyone taking the time to chat with him due to his speech being hard to understand.

Ben obviously was totally cool with it and the Aussie asked him why. Ben explained that he had been at school with a girl who had CP and he was quite used to it.

The Aussie then said that the only N.Z. girl he knew was this "hard-core boccia chick" who he'd played against a couple of times over the years.

Ben then said, "The chick at school played boccia, wouldn't be the same one, would it?"

Turned out it was the same one – me.

How small the world is that two guys can meet in a pub in Australia and I can be the topic of conversation, especially as I really didn't know either of them that well.

You really don't know how you influence people throughout your life.

Using My Voice for Good

At the sweet age of fifteen, I debuted into public speaking.

My father worked for Sport Bay of Plenty and a colleague was putting on a conference for the Kiwi Able nationwide programme. This programme was a precursor to the Halberg Disability Sports Foundation, which, as you know, I ended up working for thirteen years later.

She asked my dad if he thought I'd be willing to be a speaker at this conference. Of course Dad immediately said yes on my behalf as to him all opportunities were good opportunities and this was no exception.

The topic was to be about me and my experiences in sport. Now, not only did I get the day off school (as it was a daytime event), but I also got paid ... what could be sweeter? I was now a professional public speaker, which was going to look good on any CV.

As the day approached, the nerves set in. I couldn't have my breakfast and the butterflies were more like a swarm of bees attacking my tum. But speak I did, and as soon as I got up on stage, the nerves settled, and I launched into my speech with gusto.

I was blown away by the response. People afterwards were coming up congratulating me and saying how my speech had changed their views on disabled people.

Now, Reader, let me remind you that this was back in the days that Dribbly Wobblies were not really in the public arena as disability was only just starting to be accepted.

The insight I gave into my world was a revelation to most of my audience, and they really appreciated the opportunity to learn from me.

From my point of view, this was the first time in my life I was given the power to influence experts' thoughts and perceptions about Dribbly Wobblies. It was intoxicating.

I realised that I had something to offer and that my story was valid and worthwhile. I had a voice and people wanted to listen. I wasn't ashamed or embarrassed anymore about the way I spoke, both figuratively and literally.

During my speech, I could see in their eyes their views changing. I now was no longer the weirdo who had a crazy voice, but I was a person who had knowledge that they wanted and needed.

Dad encouraged me to accompany him to the courses he ran on coaching athletes with a disability, and I thoroughly enjoyed those sessions. I even meet people to this day who remember me from way back then. I didn't think I'd made such an impact, but apparently, I did.

My dad and I became quite a good double act. He had the knowledge about facts and figures, and I had the real-life experiences.

Dad was preparing me for my future, and we both very quickly discovered that using my voice and my experiences was the best way to change a person's perspective. He could talk about CP and sports until he was blue in the face, but the impact I gave through my speech was much more powerful. That was something he taught me and encouraged me to embrace. I have been able to utilise this skill throughout my career and still do.

Out There Talking About It

At university we had to give presentations. Obviously, one is always better with subjects that are personal, so consequently, the presentations on the subject matter that I knew all about were always my best and well received.

After I'd got back from the Sydney Paralympics, I did a lot of speaking in schools, organisations, and workplaces telling my sporting story and how I had got there. I'd like to think that I have motivated people and dispelled myths around disability.

Once I had confidence and knowledge in my career with Halberg, I began running courses by myself. Some good, some bad, and some downright funny.

One of the scenarios I would set to the groups was about fictitious little Jimmy, who uses a wheelchair and wanted to do the long jump just like his friends. I would ask them to come up with a solution to get little Jimmy involved.

On one particular occasion, it took all my strength not to wet myself with laughter when one group proudly shared their grand idea.

"Let's make a giant ramp so that Jimmy can wheel down and then at the bottom of the ramp he puts the brakes on and he flies into the sandpit. They can measure his flight and record that as a jump."

This group was actually very serious and were so excited to share this brilliant idea that it never occurred to them of the likelihood that little Jimmy could actually become more disabled as a result of this.

Some of the solutions from these groups were so crazy that it made hilarious anecdotes for the Friday night drinkies.

Another course I ran sticks in my memory for very different reasons, as it was such a classic example of pre-conceptions, assumptions, and bad attitudes.

On arrival, it was obvious that the audience had been made to attend. They all sat with arms firmly crossed, eyes rolling and with petulant expressions. The worst of these was the centre's manager, who was like the proverbial heckler at a comedian's first show.

I had my work cut out for me.

But, not being fazed, I was determined to change the atmosphere in the room, chuck in a few jokes, have a laugh at myself, and deliver an excellent three-hour workshop.

Throughout the session, the manager had only negative input, challenging me on every idea I was trying to impart.

An example of one of these was the fact that they had a gym upstairs with no lift.

He said, "We can't have gym members in wheelchairs, that's just how it is."

My response was to ask the participants, "So what can we do about that?" That really annoyed him even more as he didn't want his staff to undermine his authority by giving solutions to something he thought was non-negotiable.

The upshot was that we came up with some really creative ways of making the gym accessible to all.

By the end of the three hours, the audience, including my biggest critic, had completely transformed their attitude as they stripped outer assumptions and discovered me as a person. They understood and valued the knowledge that I was teaching them about how to become a better organisation.

Now, this was a powerful watershed moment in my career, as this was the first time that I had been in an unfriendly environment and had needed to use all my skills to convince the audience.

On reflection, these three hours were the hardest, and it was the most energy-zapping session I had ever run. As I left the building, I felt the urge to punch the air with elation. I had single-handedly changed the attitudes of twenty negative people into warm, welcoming, and unafraid human beings.

At the end of the workshop, the manager approached me and actually apologised for his negative attitude and behaviour.
I respected his honesty when he said that at the start he didn't want to be there. He told me he hadn't wanted to engage with me but by the end, he saw the value and was excited about the possibilities of the inclusion of the disability community within his organisation.
This led to working with him on an extended project, which resulted in an award-winning system at the end of two years.

It never ceased to amaze me how far this guy came, from being completely negative to a passionate and strong advocate for the disabled community. At the award ceremony, he took me to one side and was almost nostalgic telling me that he would never forget this personal journey he had been on from the day he had met me two years prior.

When I see the change in someone's attitude, it always reminds me just how powerful words are.

EPILOGUE

The Mountain

Let's go back to 'March Madness'. But first, I want to let you know that I still have places to go and mountains to climb, and so speaking of mountains ...

There is a mountain where I live that stands guard over a beautiful ocean on one side and a calm harbour on the other. It is named Mauao. This mountain has lured people from all around the world for the majestic views it offers. It draws them up onto its slopes via paths and steps in order for them to experience the magnificence and be part of the sacredness of this Māori treasure.

When I arrived in Mount Maunganui and bought an apartment in the village, my mobility had significantly deteriorated. This was to the point that I was using my wheelchair as my main form of getting around. A far cry from my uni days of walking unaided, this sedentary lifestyle had resulted in me putting on weight and being unfit. Also, my stability was crashing around me, literally. I was falling every day and, because I wasn't young anymore, the falls were resulting in major injuries, which compounded my lack of movement.

Oh, dear. Life was getting hard. Here I was in this beautiful, idyllic, beach holiday location, and I was stuck in my apartment like a prisoner looking out over the world but not being part of it. This wasn't going to end well unless I did something about it.

I had been going to a gym three times a week when I had lived in Auckland. Now, when I say, going to the gym, I was going but not necessarily giving it 100 percent. You see, I was working, so I was pretty exhausted by the time I got there which meant not being able to fully push myself.

After I had shifted to The Mount, I knew I needed to make a change, and as I had decided to 'retire', I had the time and the energy to actually push myself to get results. I asked my good mate, whom I had worked with at Halberg, if she knew of a place, and she recommended a particular gym as they had specialised equipment for disabled people. The other thing she thought was a bonus was that the staff weren't just personal trainers but qualified exercise physiologists giving them insight into the needs of their members.

My immediate reaction was "I don't think so! I'm not going to a place full of crips!" I mean, let's face it, why would I want to do that? I had always gone to mainstream gyms before and prided myself on being inclusive, so I never thought about going to somewhere 'special' (and you know what I mean by that word!).

However, I swallowed my pride and gave it a go.

For the first few weeks, I thought my trainer was rather namby pamby in his approach to my sessions. Obviously, he hadn't worked with someone like me before, hard-core. He was used to kumbaya, happy clappy crips that don't want to work too much ... and then I came along.

Once he got to know me and knew that he could push me – wow, did he push!!! He enjoyed the challenge of trying to break me (p.s. he never has). We formed a really unique and amazing bond whereby he created innovative, fantastic hard-core sessions and knew when to push and when to pull it back. I soon began to get stronger, lose some weight, and feel back in control of my world.

In the meantime, friends and family would come and stay and one of the 'must dos' was to climb The Mount. They always came home raving about the amazing sights, and I would see the photos on their Facebook and Instagram. I thought 'was this the only way I was going to see the view?'
It was at that point I asked my trainer if he reckoned I could do the climb.

By now, we had spent enough time together for him to know that I was very stubborn and was pretty unbreakable.
His answer was, "Yes, with a lot of work."
"Great, let's do it then." And so, the challenge began.

A big milestone was looming, my fortieth, and I wanted to prove to myself that not only had I brought my mobility back from the brink, but that there was still life in the old dog yet. This was a challenge I needed. After resigning from my job, moving to a new place, not knowing anyone, I was acutely afraid of fading into insignificance. I didn't realise how much being employed was tied up in ones self-worth and now that I didn't have my job family, who was I? And what did I stand for?

Mauao called my name. He knew he could provide me with purpose.

The decision had been made in November, the date the climb was to be was on my birthday (do you remember that date, Reader?), March 14. This gave us time to hone the training, specifically around what I would need in order to get me up and down. Mind you, I knew it wasn't going to be a doddle, but I was extremely confident that it wouldn't be that hard either. How delusional can you get! I sometimes forget quite how messed up my body is until I put myself into an extreme situation.

As a disabled person, you feel like you're always taking from people. I get support, I get funding for various pieces of equipment, I get home help, I get a personal trainer. I get, I get, I get. This was an opportunity for me to give back to an organisation that had given me so much. Sure, I paid for my sessions, but what I got out of them was so much more than just the physical benefits.

I got my self-worth back and to me, that's priceless.

This particular gym is a charity and therefore relies on the Trust that governs it for most of its financial support. With this in mind, I thought it would be a brilliant opportunity to use my walk as a way of raising funds for them. When we set up the funding, I hoped that I'd be able to raise $500.00, or at least ten bucks to get me a 4kg kettlebell. The gym only has the basic equipment and a 4kg kettlebell wasn't one of them. A week after the walk, it was up to $4,000.00.

So the big day dawned. It was stunning. All three of my grandparents looked down, blew the cyclone from the previous day away, parted the clouds, and demanded the sun to shine.

I arrived at the base to meet my trainers, or as I liked to call them, my pretty boys. One on each arm has to be good for the self-image and I always go with the hotties!!!

Along with the two pretty boys, I also had a towel boy who happens to be the CEO of the gym. There was a very good reason for having him come along, as once wet, the towel was snapped which resulted in it becoming ice cold. Consequently, quite frequently, I'd call out to my towel boy to get snapping. This wonderful piece of equipment was given to me by my neighbours and was such the perfect gift as I walked up the mountain.

Not only was the iced towel very welcomed but it also kept me somewhat entertained because every so often I would call over my shoulder, "Are you still enjoying the view back there, towel boy?"

Getting back to the beginning of this climb. I was totally overwhelmed by the number of people who had turned up to cheer me on. They included the brand-new leader of the Government's Opposition party along with a television news crew and local newspaper. I felt like quite the celebrity, and flashes of the Paralympics came flooding back. I was going to stretch my fifteen minutes of fame out to as long as it was going to take me to walk up and down that mountain.

I call it a mountain, well, everyone calls it a mountain when in fact it's just a big hill. It stands 232 metres high. Might not sound much ... but you try walking it with a crazy body, it soon becomes Mount Everest.

So, the walk began. I wanted to do this under my own steam, so my trainer figured out to put a specific belt around me. Now, the belt he had in mind was one used in the gym for the real crips. It was a hideous blue, from breast to hip wide with big handles for the trainers to control the wearer.
I took one look at that belt and said, "Not on your Life!!! I'm not wearing that, I want to look pretty."

So they put their heads together and came up with a five centimetre wide, colour co-ordinated strap that they could hang onto either side of me but still made it look like a fashion accessory.

First job done! Looking pretty.
Second job. Getting me up there.
Third job. Get my sore body down … literally!

Adrenaline kicked in as I was walking my first hundred metres with cameras in my face and people yelling encouragement. It was all a bit overwhelming, and I started to puff.
One of my pretty boys said, "Geez, Stace, this ain't a good sign if you're puffing already."
As we left my supporters behind to take the first set of steps, I calmed down and got into the swing of it.

My mum and dad had arrived at the base, but they wanted me to shine, so they took a different route to the top. They also said they would have the bubbles ready for me when I arrived. The thought of a glass of bubbles sustained me throughout this perilous journey.
I was concentrating so hard on my foot placement and not crossing the imaginary line with my feet that I wasn't looking up or around. So it wasn't until my trainer said, "Stop, you've got to see this." that I looked around and saw the majesty of my home from such an amazing vantage point. It took my breath away.

I was on fire. I felt really good, and I was walking at a fast pace. My trainers were surprised at how good I was going, it all felt just so right and natural and easy. HOWEVER, this feeling did not last long because as I got higher, the incline got steeper and the stairs got larger, everything got harder. The delusion disappeared, and reality set in. This was the hardest thing I'd ever done, and I was only half way to the top.

The news camera was still on me, there were also live feeds streaming to the gym's Facebook page, I had to look happy and I had to look in control. The final push to the summit was gruelling, but I knew I just had to keep putting one foot in front of another.

Finally after one hour and twenty minutes, I broke through the trees to the joyous applause of onlookers including my mum and dad. Seeing them choked me up but I managed to keep it together, raising my arms above my head, pumping my fists in the air, and using Sir Edmund Hillary's quote, I said, "I just knocked the bastard off!!!" Now I know what he must have felt like.

I was sure they would edit that bit out of the news footage, but they didn't. They probably felt assured no one would understand what I'd said anyway.

Dad popped the cork on the bubbles, which was a great sound, and while I sat there enjoying the view with glass in hand, I suddenly realised what I had accomplished. Not very often do I let myself give in to self-congratulatory emotions, but

I did then. I did this and I did this under my own steam and it felt so good.

Then reality hit … oh damn, I still had to walk down! I must admit, I was in a bit of pain. I knew what the final leg of the journey entailed and knew it was going to hurt.

At the time, I didn't know that my pretty boys had got in touch with the Surf Club who happily offered to have their four-wheel drive on call to evacuate me at any time.
So at the top, one of them said, "You've done enough, your hip is killing you I think we need to call in the cavalry."
This option was never on my radar because if I took this I would have failed. In everyone's mind, climbing up was enough, but the deal in my head was that I walk both up and down this mountain.

And so began the journey down.

Holy moly, the walk up was a doddle compared to the walk down. My body started to tell me, 'What the hell are you doing, you crazy woman? You're forty and you're going to kill us! Stop it NOW!' But I couldn't, it wasn't a choice and so I just kept going with one foot after another.

Thank goodness there were no cameras around to see the pain on my face I couldn't hide it any longer. The doubts were creeping in 'Have I got enough to do this?'

That's when my pretty boys showed their true colours. Not only were they coaching me with the physical actions, but they started using psychological tricks to take my mind off the pain such as asking me inane questions like,

"What countries have you been to, Stace?" just to keep me talking. It worked. Another beautiful thing one of the trainers said was a chant that he uses when he runs marathons. "I am a robot, I feel no pain." This was my mantra for the last twenty minutes to get me down.

As I rounded the final bend of the steps, I could see all my cheerleaders on the platform at the bottom cheering me on. That was the push I needed to complete the mission. They had my wheelchair ready, but when I arrived I knew I hadn't quite finished. This was not where I started from so this was not to be where I finished even though my body was saying 'please, please, stop'. There were still another 500 metres to go. Now, this doesn't seem like much, but I was running on empty and my wheelchair was beckoning this was the longest and slowest 500 metres of my life.

By this time, the tiredness and pain was really taking its toll, and my feet were tending to cross over with each step. I had to really concentrate on every movement.

This challenge ended on a high. Not only had I knocked the bastard off, but I did so without one fall. Mission accomplished.

However it didn't stop there.

The next day I went off to the doctor to get some anti-inflammatory pills for my hip. I limped into the surgery and was immediately recognised by both the staff and the waiting patients as a newspaper article about me was on the counter.
I stopped limping as soon the people called out their praises and proceeded to make up another excuse as to why I was there.

The same day, the T.V. reporter wanted to film some shots of me in the gym to round off the story. As I staggered in, the CEO greeted me and said that the reporter was waiting with a camera in the next room. What happened next reminded me of the final scene in the movie The Usual Suspects where Keyserr Söze limps away from the crime scene. As he gets further into the distance his limping diminishes until he is walking perfectly strong and fine. So, like Keyser, I limped towards the room, and as I got within the reporter's view, my limp and any sign of pain disappeared. I was then filmed on various pieces of gym equipment without any discomfort showing.

I got known on Facebook as well with over 3,000 likes given to that story when they posted it to their Newshub on TV3 page. I also read through some of the comments saying about how inspirational I was, which, as you've already read, doesn't sit well with me. This sparked off a robust discussion with my sister who pointed out that this is how people show their admiration for my accomplishments. But all I hear is a word that, for me, is more of a platitude used when people don't know what else to say.

A couple of weeks later my climb appeared on Newshub, on TV, one of our national news programmes.
They had interviewed Mum and Dad at the top of The Mount while waiting for me. What my parents said summed me up perfectly:

Dad: "Oh we're pretty excited actually and pretty damn proud as well."
Mum: "Yeah, we thought we'd be waiting a helluva lot longer, but she's nearly here. Not surprised though, she's so stubborn just like her father."

I then arrived, and a good camera shot was taken of Dad popping the cork from the bubbles.
Lo and behold a few days later, I went to the gym to be presented with a box from Leveret Estate Winery with two bottles of the same bubbles we had used. A lovely message that read:

> *Congratulations on your amazing achievement! You truly are an inspiration. We were delighted to see you celebrating at the top of Mauao with a bottle of Leveret IQ Brut. Keep up the great work and we*

look forward to seeing where your hard work and determination takes you next.

Warm regards
Abbie Davie
Cellar Door Manager.

Wow … How cool is that!! My celebrity lives on.

There was a dual reason why I climbed Mauao that day. The sheer satisfaction of achieving something big and supporting a charity dear to my heart.
I'm pleased to say I accomplished both.
I am astonished at how many people got behind it. People I did and didn't know reached into their pockets and donated generously. It was exciting to be part of the decision-making process about what equipment we would purchase.

I got my 4kg kettlebell and a truckload more!
This is just the beginning of the next chapter of my life, which I'm actually very excited about.

Keep a lookout, Reader, for the next instalment.

THE PERSONAL SCRIBBLER SPEAKS

Having known Stacey since she was a teenager, it was a no-brainer to me that she should write her story. It started on a beautiful day when we met up again after a few years' absence. While enjoying a wonderful lunch, I asked her, "Why don't you write your memoirs?"
She replied, "I would if I could, but physically can't."

Now, being an author and knowing how compelling it is to get that story out of your head, it seemed only logical to respond, "What say we meet once a week for coffee, I'll bring my laptop, you talk, and I'll type?"

How little did I know just what an amazingly awesome journey I was about to have hanging out with this fabulously corker lady. She has taken me on a ride filled with peeing laughter to shedding emotional tears, falling off chairs because of the hilarity or grabbing the tissues for both of us as we headed full tilt through this life of hers.

I started off as a simple ghostwriter because it was something I had done before, but when Stacey gave me the title of 'Personal Scribbler', I knew she'd made me part of her life and for that she will remain in my heart forever.

- Fee ♥

THE END ... FOR NOW

Now you can close this book and lets all sing ...

♫♪♪ Kumbaya ♫♪♪